Presented
Nyack C   y
by
Ben and Ruth Freed
Armstrong

REACHING ARABS FOR CHRIST

In honor of my father
Ralph Freed '25
March 1998

RALPH FREED, D.D.
General Director
Trans World Radio

REACHING ARABS FOR CHRIST

By
RALPH FREED

Trans World Radio

560 MAIN STREET
CHATHAM, N. J. USA

1972

REACHING ARABS FOR CHRIST
Amplified Edition
Copyright 1972
Trans World Radio

Original Edition Copyright 1947
Reprinted by permission
Zondervan Publishing House
Grand Rapids, Michigan

Printed in the U.S.A.
1972

9006672

Foreword

It was in 1947 that my book entitled *Reaching Arabs for Christ* was first published.

Twenty-five years have passed since then. A strong desire has been expressed by my son and others to reprint this account of personal ministries among the Arabs over the period of 21 years from 1926 to 1946.

This book will take you to the Arabs, a race of people very little known or heard of by the average Christian in connection with the preaching of the Gospel. The Gospel labors among them are difficult—yet not without fruit.

In order to place these years of ministries in the Near East in right perspective, I am adding two opening and three closing chapters to the book. The two chapters entitled Prologue relate the background of my conversion, my call to the missionary ministry, and the actual beginning of my missionary career.

The three closing chapters entitled Epilogue link the ending of my missionary work in the Arab lands to the Lord's wonderful guidance to join my son Paul and start together a Gospel radio ministry. This led us in 1954 to Tangier, North Africa, to reach Spain with the Gospel, then on to Monte Carlo in 1960 to broadcast eventually in 35 languages to targets in Europe, North Africa and the Middle East. In 1964 another wonderfully effective door was opened in the building of a most powerful station in Bonaire, Netherlands Antilles, in the Caribbean area, from where we broadcast to North and South America, Europe, and India.

While the Epilogue of this book touches only very briefly this radio ministry during the period of the past 18 years, the story is related fully and most interestingly in my son's book entitled *Towers to Eternity* published in 1968.

1972
Monte Carlo, Monaco

Introduction

Early in the year 1936 it was the great privilege of my wife, daughter and I to visit Palestine and other countries in the Near East. When we arrived in Jerusalem we were received as guests of Pastor and Mrs. Freed at the American Gospel Church on the Street of the Prophets.

It was with a peculiar feeling of delight that we settled down there for several days and enjoyed a time of real fellowship with these devoted servants of the Lord. While Mrs. Freed did everything possible to minister to our comfort in the home, her husband proved to be an indefatigable and well-informed guide, taking us from place to place of interest to tourists and Bible students and giving us a vast amount of information that otherwise we would have missed. To stand in his pulpit and preach the Gospel by interpretation to Jews and Arabs alike was a heart-moving opportunity of which I was glad to avail myself on several occasions.

I learned to regard these consecrated missionaries very highly indeed, and I am happy to have the privilege of writing a few words of commendation of the book now before the reader. I feel sure it will be used of God to awaken many to a prayerful interest in the Arabs of Palestine, the Hauran and the entire Near East. To see conditions as they are, through the eyes of Pastor Freed, will mean to many Christians a new conception of our responsibility to give to the sons of Ishmael that precious Gospel which the sons of Isaac originally gave to us. It is only as we thus become familiar with conditions that our spirits are stirred to pray and do what we can for the salvation of many people. Too long the impression has prevailed among Christians in western lands that Arabs are practically impervious to the message of the Evangel. Mr. Freed's book gives many proofs to the contrary and ought to be an encouragement to us all to count on God to open the eyes of those so long blinded by the delusions of the false prophet Mohammed and enable them to see the beauty and glory of our Lord Jesus, the one Mediator between God and man.

H. A. IRONSIDE

Chicago, Illinois

CONTENTS

CHAPTER 1

Prologue I

MILDRED, our little baby Paul, and I were a contented family in Detroit, Michigan. I not only had a good job, but a very interesting one. Working for the Burroughs Adding Machine Company, I always had the ambition to go beyond what my daily work required. In my spare time I learned the technical and mechanical intricacies of the many designs of accounting and bookkeeping machines. I gave a great deal of study to the many supplementary devices offered by the company. I realized that one of the things needful in this large organization was the knowledge of how to select the right combination of equipment for the bookkeeping and general accounting needs of various large corporations, be it a bank, an insurance company, an auto

11

manufacturer or a railroad line. Gradually I made myself
a specialist along these lines and a much-sought-for advisor
to my company.

We had been faithful church members in the Methodist
church of a residential suburb of Birmingham, Michigan, and
so our lives were carefree and self-satisfied.

Everything went without any special event until one Sunday in 1920 our pastor made an announcement of seemingly
little significance. That announcement, however, caused a
complete change in our lives. In making his usual remarks
this Sunday morning, he added: "In the old Town Hall down
the street, I understand they are to have some special meetings by a group of religious fanatics. I warn you not to get
involved in those meetings!" We probably would not even
have taken notice of these special meetings had not our pastor
called attention to them.

That afternoon we passed by the old Town Hall and
noticed newly painted banners telling of the forthcoming
meetings. We were particularly struck by a large banner
stretched over the entrance with only two words on it,
"JESUS SAVES."

In the meantime a neighbor lady, whom we knew only in
passing, called on Mildred and gave her a hearty invitation
to attend the special meetings. In the course of the conversation the subject of that banner came up. The visiting lady
realized right away Mildred's sincerity on one hand, but also
her total ignorance of the true meaning and significance of
the Gospel as applied to her personal life. Our pastor had
been faithfully giving us the social implications of Christianity so-called, but never said a word about the need of personal salvation. The words of this lady left a deep impression

on Mildred's mind, and all week she pondered the things she had heard.

In the meantime the special meetings in the Town Hall started. One evening Mildred said to me, "Ralph, why don't you go to the Hall and try to find out what is going on there?" So I did. The Hall had large but high, plain glass windows. I went around the building in the dark until, under one of the windows, I found a large stone just big enough for me to stand on and look through the window.

It was prayer time. I thought it was strange that one person after the other from the congregation stood up and led in prayer. Some prayed awfully long, I thought. I was used to hearing only the pastor offer his usual Sunday morning or evening pastoral prayer. This in the Hall was quite different. I went home and reported what I had observed. This made Mildred think even more. A few days later she suggested that we slip into the meeting and see and hear for ourselves. This we did, and for the remaining week of special meetings, we attended faithfully. I was interested but nothing more. I did not have any idea of the deep conviction that was going on in Mildred's heart until the closing meeting of the campaign.

The meeting room, holding possibly 80 to 100 people, was full and we could only find a place quite close to the front, right on the center aisle. The evangelist gave another message. As usual, at the close he invited anyone who wanted to accept the Lord as his or her personal Saviour to come forward and kneel in the front row of chairs, which were kept free for this purpose.

I was sitting next to the aisle and Mildred next to me. Suddenly she gave me a gentle push and said, "Please let me get out." Immediately I realized what she was about to do. So I started to whisper to her, "Please, when we get home, let's talk things over. I realize we ought to do better and be more faithful in our church attendance; we ought to perhaps give more money to the Church. . . ." Mildred didn't even hear what I said, she was under such deep conviction of sin. She pushed past me and the next thing I saw was her kneeling by one of the front-row chairs, her face buried. When I saw her there, a thought came to me as a bolt from heaven almost in an audible voice, "If Mildred is a sinner and needs salvation, what about you?" The next moment I was on my way to the front and knelt beside Mildred. That evening both of us were wonderfully saved.

For the next few weeks we attended the meetings at the Town Hall but also were present in our church from time to time. We were not happy about this and discussed how we could most gracefully withdraw from the church. The Lord solved this problem for us.

It was a Saturday, and we were in the shopping center of Birmingham when we suddenly confronted our pastor. He stepped up to us and spoke to us rather coldly, "I understand, Mr. and Mrs. Freed, that you have been frequenting those Town Hall meetings of late and have been neglecting your church." Mildred was of a naturally shy nature, but to my surprise she spoke up before I even could think what to answer. "Yes, Dr. S., we have been attending the Town Hall and there the Lord saved our souls!" There was a long silence. Then the pastor turned to us and said, "I thought before, that you two were intelligent people, but I am shocked!" Then he tipped his hat and said goodbye. That was the last time we saw him.

Chapter 2

Prologue II

M Y work with the Burroughs Adding Machine Company continued. I was thinking of it in terms of a lifetime position, being encouraged by my steady financial progress.

Having been converted, I sought out all opportunities to witness to friends of my new-found faith. Among those of my business associates to whom I had opportunity to witness was a Mr. F., about 20 years my senior. He was in charge of the general mailing department and from time to time would drop into my office not only to attend to business but to have a personal chat with me. I used such opportunities to witness to him. He listened, but did not seem to be much impressed. As a matter of fact, while a church member, he did not be-

lieve much of anything concerning spiritual things but rather
scoffed at them.

On one such occasion Mr. F. stood in front of my desk, and
we were chatting about things in general. Suddenly he turned
to me and pointing his finger at me said, "Ralphie, do you
really believe all the stuff you have been telling me about
salvation and that every man has to accept Christ to get to
heaven?" I looked into his face and said, "Yes, I believe it
with all my heart." He stepped even closer to me and said,
"Ralphie, if you believe that the heathen in Africa and Asia
who have never heard the Gospel are hopelessly lost, and you
are satisfied to sit here in your comfortable office and draw
your salary, you are the biggest hypocrite I ever knew!" I
was shocked and did not know what to say. Finally I said,
"Thank you," and he left my office.

That night I slept very little, pondering over this startling
accusation. I went back to my office next morning, but it did
not look the same and my big arm chair did not seem as
comfortable as before.

Mildred and I prayed about the challenge of this uncon-
verted man and gradually came to the conclusion that the
Lord was speaking to us. Some weeks later I put in my resignation with the thought of going to a Bible College and then
applying for missionary service. Soon I was drawn in my
thinking to the Arab lands of the Near East.

When my immediate superior received my resignation, he
passed it on to the President of the Burroughs Company. A
few days later I was surprised to have the President's Special
Assistant personally come to my office. Since Burroughs was
a large organization of over a thousand employees at the
headquarters offices besides the ten thousand workers in the

factory, his visit was a rare occurrence. Mr. S. told me that the President was taking a special interest in me. He felt that if I was interested in living abroad, they could arrange the establishment of a branch office in the country and place of my own choosing, knowing that I could develop a profitable business for the company.

I told Mr. S. that I was very grateful to the President for his kind offer, but my desire to go abroad was not for a change of location but that the Lord was calling me to preach the Gospel to the Arabs.

By this time the Lord had given us also a baby girl, Ruth, and on January 1, 1924, we arrived at Nyack, New York, at the Missionary Training College. Space will not permit me to tell you of all the precious experiences the Lord permitted us to have during the next two and a half years. I will mention only one aspect of the lessons the Lord was to teach us in Nyack.

I had a good salary at Burroughs, but feeling that I had a secure position, we did not try to save much money but gave generously to foreign missions. When I had made the decision to resign and on short notice went to Nyack, I had only a few hundred dollars saved. Though this amount would normally have been sufficient for our living expenses for only two or three months, the Lord definitely led us not to say a word to anyone about our financial situation.

The obvious impression I must have left with the faculty members and students was that, giving up such a fine position, I would undoubtedly be well taken care of financially for the two years of training which I planned to undertake. Suffice it to say that the Lord permitted us several times to have the last loaf of bread and very little else in the cupboard, not knowing where food would come from the next day to feed a family of four. But God is faithful, and it was a joyful experience to see how He laid burdens on hearts to meet our needs. He never failed us.

After having completed my studies, we were appointed by the Board of the Christian and Missionary Alliance to their established work in the Near East. It was a memorable day when, in October 1926, we sailed for the field, known at that time as the Palestine and Arabian Border field.

So I have brought you, dear reader, to the point where the following chapters will tell you of the blessed ministries the Lord granted to us. These subsequent chapters, apart from the closing chapters entitled "Epilogue," were previously published in 1947.

CHAPTER 3

Prelude

... waters in the wilderness ... (Isaiah 43:20).

WE were traveling through "no man's land," an arid, barren country at the junction of Northern Palestine, Lebanon and Syria. There was only dirt and stone with no trace of vegetation as far as one could see—and that was not very far at times because of the cloud of dust which literally enveloped our car as it made its way slowly on the rugged trail.

After miles of travel without seeing a human being, we suddenly passed an Arab shepherd boy leading his flock of sheep. We went quite a distance past them when the thought struck us that the presence of the shepherd boy un-

19

doubtedly indicated that there must be water not too far away. We turned around. By the time we reached the shepherd, another thought was going through my mind and I immediately shared it with Mr. Brooks, my missionary companion. "We must be near the source of the Jordan, perhaps within walking distance," I said.

We inquired from the Arab boy about water and he led us to a very small brook, a mere crack in the ground, with a bare trickle of water winding its way like a ribbon through the open field. We were disappointed. The shepherd boy, noticing our wondering expression, said, "Much, much water over there," and pointed to a black spot in the far distance. His trained eyes could easily see it, though it took us a while before we detected it. We knew that such a spot indicated either a Bedouin encampment with its black goat-hair tents, or an oasis with its green vegetation which appears black from a distance. "Much, much water . . ." gave us encouragement that it might be what we were looking for.

After a long wearisome walk through stony fields, we reached our objective and stood gazing with fascination at a large cluster of lovely trees. There was a grove which covered an acre. Unless you have been in desert country, you cannot appreciate, as we do in the Near East, what trees mean in the midst of barrenness. There is something delightful and exhilarating about them. The contrast makes us value them the way we never do where vegetation is plentiful.

In the direction from which we came we saw no sign of water, and this made the presence of the trees rather mysterious. We pierced through the outer rows of trees and to our surprise we saw that the grove surrounded a large pool of water. "A pool of water!" we both exclaimed in astonishment, for we saw no trace of a spring anywhere. But as we looked at the pool, we discovered that there were bubbles all over the surface of it. On closer observation we noticed that the water was bubbling and stirring the way it boils in a kettle. Then we understood. It sprang from an underground source, and the source itself was swallowed up in the pool it had formed. On the other end of the pear-shaped pool we saw the outlet—a crystal-clear stream flowing southward.

Now we looked to the north, and above the tree tops we saw in the far distance—nearly a hundred miles away— snow-capped Mount Hermon towering above all the other ranges. Then the secret and the wonder of it all fully unfolded to our hearts and minds. The perennial snows of Mount Hermon melted and disappeared underground; then, far away, in the midst of barren desolation and depressing heat, this hidden stream broke forth, bringing life in its wake.

* * *

What a picture this is of the spiritual history of the Holy Land! It depicts the Gospel sent down from heaven, then disappearing in the centuries of desert darkness and finally breaking forth anew in our day.

The average Christian, when thinking of Palestine and the Near East, readily recalls the shining forth of the glorious light of the Gospel with the coming of Christ, and is familiar with the marvelous and rapid flow of the streams of salvation as recorded in the book of Acts.

Comparatively few Christians realize, however, that the ancient Bible lands, which at the close of the first century of the Christian era had scores of churches and tens of thousands of born-again believers, have become with the passing of centuries spiritually parched. Today the Near East is one of the neediest mission fields of the world.

The next chapter will relate what happened to Christianity in Bible lands in the course of the centuries from the end of recorded Bible history till our day, and how the Gospel light turned to awful darkness and the streams of salvation to spiritual barrenness and desolation.

CHAPTER 4

Retrospect

If . . . the light that is in thee be darkness . . . (Matthew 6:23).

S ACRED history, as recorded in the Word of God, comes
to an abrupt end with the account of the Apostle Paul's
preaching and teaching in Rome (Acts 28:30-31). His
expected martyrdom seems to be alluded to in one of his
epistles (II Timothy 4:6). The time is about 66 A.D. Let
us now take up the thread of history from secular sources.

As the result of an uprising of the Jews against Rome
in 66 A.D., led by Gessius Florus, the Roman general Ves-
pasian and later Titus were sent with a formidable army
to put down the rebellion. Jerusalem and a few other places
resisted. Consequently, Jerusalem was stormed and captured

23

in September, 70 A.D. In spite of the express order of Titus, the Temple was destroyed and only small portions of the city were left standing. The destruction of Jerusalem was followed by the dispersion of the Jews into Galilee and the neighboring provinces, and, with the passing of centuries, throughout the countries of Europe. Only a handful of God's chosen people were left in ancient Bible lands.

At the close of the apostolic records we find the Christian churches in Palestine, Syria and in the lands beyond the Jordan growing in number and in spiritual strength. As the political persecutions caused the scattering of the Jews throughout these Eastern provinces, so likewise the religious persecutions of the Jewish Christians caused them to be scattered even more. Wherever they went the message of the Gospel was faithfully proclaimed. As time went on an increasing number of heathen Gentiles were obedient to the Word. With the Temple gone we now find Christianity separating more and more from even an outward conformity to Jewish rites and customs, and a distinct Christian Church organization, form and ritual beginning to develop—as yet pure and true in its principle and practice.

At the end of the second century Christian churches are well established in several hundred cities and towns of importance in the Near East (beside those in Europe), and reach into Persia to the east and into Arabia to the south.

The attitude of the Roman Government during the two hundred years following the apostolic era varied from passive antagonism to most violent persecution, and many a Christian gained, amid the most horrible tortures, the martyr's crown. In spite of this the Church steadily grew until in 311 the Emperor Galerius upon his deathbed granted it toleration; and in 313 the Emperor Constantine published the famous edict of Milan, proclaiming complete religious liberty and making Christianity a legal religion.

Constantine, recognizing the growing strength of the Church and wishing to enlist the support of the Christians treated them with increasing favor and finally was himself baptized upon his deathbed (337). Under Theodosius the Great, in 385, Christianity was established as the sole religion of the Roman State and heathen worship was put under ban. Thus the union of State and Church came about and continued in the East until the rise of Islam. The division into the Eastern and Western Empires in the seventh century brought about the division of the Church but was not made official until 1054. It completely separated the Greek Catholic (Eastern) and Roman Catholic (Western) Churches.

The beginning of royal favors under Constantine was, of course, the beginning of the departure from the purity of the Early Church. More and more formalism and pagan practices crept into the Christian worship and the ban under which heathen worship was placed by subsequent emperors was of little significance to the populace since paganism in an altered form was freely offered in State Christianity. Prof. Harnack puts it in this way: "Paganism was not extirpated but simply absorbed."

Amid the churches of the Orient there was for a period (from the fifth to the seventh centuries) a revival of a comparatively pure evangelical faith in the Nestorian Church, which spread in parts of the Eastern lands and sent missionaries as far as China. The remnants of the Nestorian Church in subsequent centuries fell into the ways of the other Oriental sects.

The long interval of political tranquillity came abruptly to an end in 611 when Chosroes II, king of Persia, invaded

Syria and Palestine, and carried plunder and destruction everywhere. Jerusalem was taken; the Church of the Holy Sepulcher was destroyed and its treasures carried off; other churches were likewise razed and the patriarch was taken prisoner. The Roman emperor Heraclius reconquered the lost territory in 628 but his triumph was short lived. A more formidable enemy, the Arabs, were on the way to wrest finally Syria, Palestine and Mesopotamia from the tottering Roman Empire.

The scattered Arab tribes of the desert—the descendents of Ishmael—unified under a new leader, Mohammed, and inspired by the new religion of Islam, emerged from oblivion about 635. Fired with an unparalleled zeal and fanaticism they started their conquests to bring the whole world—at the point of the sword—to the worship of Allah alone and of his prophet Mohammed.

His successor, Abu-Bekr, marched northward to capture the fertile provinces of Palestine and Syria from the infidel dogs, the Christians. The Byzantine emperor Heraclius was defeated and Abu-Bekr seized Bosra and began the siege of Damascus. Upon his death he was succeeded by the Moslem conqueror Omar, who took the city. Other towns were captured in turn—Caesarea, Samaria, Jaffa and finally Jerusalem—and so the Byzantine Empire in Syria and Palestine fell into the hands of the Arabs. Omar's terms of peace offered full liberty and equality to all who would become Mohammedans, but on the rest humiliating terms were laid. Omar took the Holy Rock, Mount Moriah—the site of the Temple and of the later Christian Church—and on its ruins built a Moslem place of worship, which though later rebuilt still bears his name (Mosque of Omar).

In 1072 Palestine was invaded by the Mohammedan Turks

who wrested power from the Arab rulers. Of course, Moslem supremacy was retained in the Near East. Waves of persecution and of massacres broke out at intervals on the least provocation on the part of the churches of the East, and these have continued till our day.

When we read of the persecutions of the Christians by the Moslem majorities, it would be a mistake to consider them equal to the persecutions of the early Christians who faced suffering and death for their personal love and devotion to Christ. Christianity, after Constantine, deteriorated to a national, racial and religious-political movement in the East. And so the persecutions and the resistance to them were more in the nature of a racial and national struggle for existence, though the underlying causes were religious.

The sufferings of these nominal Christian groups at the hand of the Moslem conquerors created widespread indignation in Europe and resulted in the crusades of the eleventh, twelfth and thirteenth centuries.

The crusades had the very same political-religious aspect to which reference was made in the foregoing paragraph. Among the many crusades, the outstanding one was that led by Godfrey of Bulloigne, in 1099, who captured Jerusalem and was made King of Jerusalem.

So was founded the Latin Kingdom of Jerusalem. For its appraisal I wish to quote from the writings of Dr. F. M. Stetson, Professor of History, University of Reading:

> The history of this kingdom is one of the most painful ever penned. It is a record of almost unredeemed envy, hatred and malice, and vice with its consequent diseases, all rendered the more repulsive in that its transactions were carried on in the name of Christianity. For eighty-eight turbulent years this feudal kingdom was imposed

on Palestine and Syria and then it disappeared as suddenly as it came, leaving no trace but ruins, a few place names and an undying hatred of Christianity among the Moslem Arab population.

Subsequent history is full of conquests by various rival Moslem races with the persistent destruction of Christian "Holy Places." Finally, in 1516, the victorious Moslem Turks established undisputed lordship over the almost purely Arab population of the Bible lands, including Mesopotamia, Arabia and Egypt. From that time on until World War I in 1914, there was practically no political change and the annals of those centuries record little save the sanguinary quarrels of local shieks. More and more the rights of the various Oriental churches, divided into numerous groups, were recognized by the sultans, though there were periods of return to persecutions and massacres.

The great Reformation and the revival of true Bible Christianity which swept Europe in the sixteenth century never touched the Orient and Bible lands remained predominantly Moslem, while the remnant of the Eastern churches continued its corrupt, idolatrous form of worship. And so the message of the reformers, the true Gospel of the grace of God, did not reach the Near East until the modern missionary movement brought it back to its shores in the latter part of the nineteenth century.

The dawn of modern world-wide missions faced the challenge of ancient Bible lands with their mixed and antagonistic population, representing the three so-called "Great Monotheistic Faiths"—Judaism, Christianity and Islam; indeed the Near East is the cradle of all three.

There we find the Jews—the sons of Israel—for centuries only a small group of bigoted Oriental Jews. However, during the past twenty-five years this number has been supplemented by more than a half million modern, cultured, Jews from all parts of the Western world.

The Arabs of the Near East—the sons of Ishmael—are conservatively estimated at sixteen million, of whom one million live in Palestine. Thus they make up two-thirds of the population of that country. As we have seen, they are either Moslem or Orthodox-Catholic.* Saudi Arabia, which is still closed to the Gospel, has an estimated population of eight million—entirely Moslem. The countries of Palestine, Transjordan, Syria and Iraq account for the other eight million Arabs of whom about 90 per cent are Moslem and 10 per cent Orthodox-Catholic. The Moslem Arabs represent perhaps the most defying challenge to the messenger of the Gospel, while the Orthodox-Catholic Arabs in their deplorable moral and spiritual state and bigoted opposition to the Gospel are a close second to their Moslem neighbors.

This is the challenge which meets the missionary in Bible lands—the challenge of backslidden Judaism that turned from the truth of the Gospel; of corrupt, bigoted Christianity

---

* The term "Orthodox-Catholic Arabs" will be used in this book, instead of the usual designation of "Christian Arabs," to indicate the adherents of the various Oriental churches. They are divided into many sects, according to geographical location and racial background, such as Greek Orthodox, Greek Catholic, Maronites, Assyrian Orthodox (Jacobites), Assyrian Catholic (Chaldeans), Copts, Syriac, etc. Some of these sects are under the pope and Rome, others are independent patriarchates. However, their doctrines and practices, with slight variations, are equally corrupt. They all consider and call themselves Arabs (Ibn 'Arab) though evidently of more mixed racial strain than the Moslems in whose midst they live as fully mingled economically and socially as the Catholics and Protestants of America.

that makes void the truth of the Gospel; of fanatical, ruthless Islam that denies the truth of the Gospel.

But what is impossible with man is possible with God and the Gospel is still the power of God unto salvation. Souls are being saved and indigenous churches are springing up again in Bible lands as we shall see in subsequent chapters. Streams are beginning to flow once more in dry river beds.

CHAPTER 5

"He... Giveth Songs in the Night"

THE years of the great riots in Palestine (1936-39) were disheartening in every respect. For Gospel ministries those days were doubly difficult. The minds of the people were so saturated with the events of the day and with the issues involved that it seemed well nigh impossible to approach them on any other subject. Even the believers were engrossed in the sorrows of that period. Besides the mental attitude of the people, general conditions made the holding of meetings more difficult month after month. For nearly three years the curfew in the cities eliminated all evening services. In cities like Jerusalem or Haifa, where the numerous Jewish and Arab settlements are as close together as the pieces of a patchwork quilt, the holding of any kind of service in any part of the city became a real problem because of the necessity for many of the people to pass through sections of the city inhabited by the other race, where they would take their lives in their own hands.

For some time the Lord burdened Mrs. Freed and myself to pray for revival in Jerusalem, but as the riots grew in intensity we knew, or at least thought we knew, that answer to our prayer would have to await some future day when everything quieted down and at least we would not have these abnormal and discouraging handicaps.

It was the winter of 1938 and the riots were at their peak. In addition, it was cold and rainy and at such times even our own Arab believers found it difficult to attend the regular meetings. Suddenly a young American evangelist, Mr. Clifford Lewis, appeared on the scene. We have had many evangelists before and since. We thoroughly enjoy our American preacher friends and have been greatly blessed by their ministries. Normally their primary purpose is—and rightly so—the visiting of places of Biblical interest, and they want to make the most of their time since these visits in the Holy Land are often limited to a few days or, very rarely, a few weeks. If they are able to spare the time, we try to have them preach to our Arabic or English-speaking congregations and their ministries are always a special treat.

How our young evangelist friend ever managed to enter Palestine in the face of the many restrictions of those days I do not know. He found out very soon that he was taking terrible risks even in trying to travel from the port city to Jerusalem. To our great amazement his first remark after we had exchanged greetings at our mission headquarters was that if he could be a help to us in holding revival services he would be glad. His offer seemed almost ridiculous. Revival services at such a time? Impossible! Yet, had we not been praying for a revival for a long time? We did not know what to do. Finally we agreed that we three would spend a good deal of time in prayer each day for a week to get the mind of the Lord.

By the time the week was over we were convinced that the Lord had sent the brother to us for the very purpose of holding revival services. But how to start to arrange for special meetings we did not know. Finally the Lord showed us to use what we had. Mrs. Freed had been conducting—in English—a small Bible class for girls. There were in that class four or five Arab girls, three Russian, one Swedish, one English—in all about twelve girls between the ages of fifteen and twenty. None of the girls were saved but all of them were very much interested in this Sunday afternoon Bible class and even the riots did not keep them from faithfully attending. So the Lord showed us that we should take one step at a time and turn the next Sunday afternoon class into an evangelistic service where our preacher brother could readily minister.

Sunday afternoon Mrs. Freed's class of girls came, in spite of the violence in the city. The meeting was held as usual in the large sitting room of the mission house which was heated, for the wind and driving rain penetrated the stone walls and cement floors. When the message was only partly finished, a deep conviction suddenly came upon one of the two Russian sisters present. She began to sob and cry; then, disregarding everyone, she jumped up and went to her sister. She threw her arms around her neck and wept and pleaded to forgive her for all her meanness to her. This unexpected act broke the heart of the sister and she also began to weep, and asked forgiveness for her mistreatment of the younger sister.

This touching scene seemed to send an arrow of conviction into the hearts of all the girls. They had been taught regularly for a year or more in the truth of the Gospel but somehow it had never reached the heart before. Truly we saw a real demonstration of the Word: "When he [the Holy Spirit] is come, he will reprove . . ." Soon we were all on our knees, and three of us were dealing with the girls, though they did not need much dealing, for the Holy Spirit had already done that and the truth which they had been taught week in and week out, was being applied by the faithful Holy Spirit. That afternoon every one of the girls prayed for salvation and received the Lord.

That was a glorious start. But what next? The Lord quickly showed us to continue as we had begun. We informed the girls that we would hold week-day meetings at three o'clock in the afternoon in the sitting room. This was the first public notice of the coming meetings. We could not make any further announcement since there was no evening service because of the curfew.

We faced the Monday afternoon service with misgivings. Who could possibly come on such a day? Maybe two or three, we thought. But they came! All the girls were there and five or six others whom they had invited. We had a blessed service. On Tuesday, in spite of heavy rains, the attendance increased to about twenty-five and we were greatly surprised. The following day we had thirty out.

Now we began to rearrange the sitting room. We removed some of the large armchairs and brought in straight chairs from the church auditorium. The sitting room seemed to be the Lord's place. Besides, we could heat it easily and make it comfortable. Day by day the weather became worse but it was evident that God's blessing was on the meetings for the attendance continued to increase.

Just about this time violence in the city was breaking out afresh. Shortly after sunset the bandits would move toward the city; they crept through the surrounding hills and valleys and shots would ring out from every direction. So to set the people at ease, we announced daily that we would see to it that the meetings would end before sunset—early enough to allow everyone to get home before the shooting began. A strange inducement, you will say, to get the people to come, but the Lord was in our midst in mighty power.

During the second week of these afternoon meetings, the attendance went up to fifty, then sixty, then seventy. By this time we had moved all the extra furniture from the sitting room and had opened up the adjoining room, too. The Lord was saving souls every day.

When at the end of three weeks we closed the special meetings we had more than two score young people gloriously saved—young people who by actual count represented twenty-two different nationalities. We in America who are accustomed to large numbers might not appreciate the import of the above, but for Jerusalem it was one of the most gracious and blessed visitations of God and it reached far and wide in the city. Nor was the blessing a passing flare-up. These young people continued in fellowship and went about everywhere witnessing for the Lord.

Today, years after the meetings, the blessings still continue and the Lord is adding to the number. Some of those who were saved have gone to other parts of Palestine and beyond the seas, but we still receive news of the deep, enduring work of the Spirit of God abiding in their hearts and lives.

Does the day seem hard? Does it appear, because of adverse circumstances, that the handicaps for God's working are too great? Maybe you say: "Yes, He might work someday, but it cannot be expected now. Everything is against it. It is too dark . . ." Remember—He giveth "songs in the night" (Job 35:10).

CHAPTER 6

"For the Love of Christ Constraineth..."

IT was a beautiful spring morning in Jerusalem in the year 1938. The fields to the south of the city toward Bethlehem were covered with lovely wild flowers, particularly with anemones—the flowers considered by many to be the lilies of the field spoken of by our Lord.

We were enjoying the hospitality of a Christian Arab friend who lived a distance from the Bethlehem road, away from the noise of the city. As we sat on the veranda and enjoyed the beautiful view of Jerusalem, a little more than two miles to the north of us, we could hear occasional shots and the shrieking sound of ambulance sirens. The land of Palestine was torn by division and bitter strife. Shots and bomb explosions, and in their wake suffering and death,

37

were a daily occurrence in the City of Peace. Military and police patrols, armored cars, searches, curfew, arrests, executions—all seemed to be of little avail for a period of nearly four years.

All the efforts of years—both by the British Government and also, in a measure, by the parties involved—to bring better understanding and co-operation between Jews and Arabs were shattered overnight. Now, as I was visiting my Arab friend, in the third year of the riots, bitterness and antagonism were so great that an Arab's life was not safe if he showed even a sign of friendliness toward any Jew, and of course a Jew would be considered a traitor if he fraternized an Arab.

It was this very condition that brought me to risk the dangers of even such a little excursion to visit this brother believer, Ishag, in order that I might fellowship with him in his trials and bring encouragement and comfort. Ishag loved the Lord Jesus Christ very dearly and there was no room in his heart for hatred even toward those who were so bitterly hated by his own kith and kin. Being a Government employee he was already under suspicion and his kindness toward the Jewish employees was soon reported to rebel headquarters. He lived quite a distance from the city in an isolated spot surrounded by a large orchard and thus was an easy target.

Only a few days before my visit, someone had come to his home in the middle of the night. He went to the door and asked who the visitor was. A stranger demanded that he open the door. When he refused several shots were fired through various windows of his house. He realized the situation. His house was surrounded by bandits. Then the man who had called him to the door and who seemed to be

the leader of the band warned him that unless he gave up his
position with the Government, changed his present attitude
and threw his whole heart into their cause, he would be
killed, his house would be blown to pieces and his wife and
seven children would be left paupers. With that warning
they said they would give him a few days to think the matter
over, and then left.

He sent word to me and you can understand how our
hearts were burdened for this brave soldier of Jesus Christ.
Now as he and I visited, our conversation naturally turned
from grim present-day realities toward future hopes. Brother
Ishag brought out his Arabic Bible, opened the blessed Book
to the sixty-second chapter of Isaiah and read: " 'For Zion's
sake will I not hold my peace, and for Jerusalem's sake I
will not rest, until the righteousness thereof go forth as
brightness, and the salvation thereof as a lamp that burneth
. . . I have set watchmen upon thy walls, O Jerusalem,
which shall never hold their peace day or night: ye that
make mention of the Lord, keep not silence, and give him
no rest, till he establish, and till he make Jerusalem a praise
in the earth.' "

He laid down the Book, looked at me and with a joyful
exclamation said: "Brother Freed, isn't that wonderful?
I believe the day is coming very soon when Jerusalem and
the Jews will be a praise in the earth. I long to see the day
when they will accept Christ as their Messiah and their
sufferings will be all over."

* * *

The riots made separation between Jews and Arabs complete. Even old friends would not dare to show their friend-

ship lest they be seen by the extremists and their lives would
not be safe.

Years ago one of our Arab believers, a man of unusual
abilities, although he was totally blind, befriended two
blind Jewish men. Misfortune brought them together. But
now during the riots they had to discontinue their periodical
visits. Some two years passed by in this way. Brother
Jameel, the Arab Christian, was very anxious to renew his
acquaintance with these men and so we arranged a meeting
on neutral ground, in our mission home. First our Arab
brother came, afterward the two Jewish men. They talked
about past days and the present awful conditions.

Our Arab brother's heart was burning with longing to
witness to his Jewish friends. He asked for portions of
the Bible in Braille and while he read from the book of
Isaiah on his lap (in the touch system for the blind each
book of the Bible is a large volume), one of the Jewish men
was following him on the pages of the Gospel of John. I
slipped into the room quietly. The picture of the three men
with the books before them is one I can never forget.
Brother Jameel was unfolding the truth concerning their
Messiah and his Saviour the Lord Jesus Christ. How I
praised the Lord that afternoon for the miracle-working
power of the Gospel in filling the heart of this Arab brother
with love for his natural enemies! "If any man be in Christ,
he is a new creature."

* * *

I wish to relate another incident to show how wonderfully
God worked in the hearts of Arab believers during those
tragic days. The day of the outbreak of the riots in Jaffa
and Tel Aviv was one of the most awful days of all. Jaffa

and Tel Aviv are twin cities. In Jaffa live about fifty-thousand Arabs and in Tel Aviv, which immediately joins Jaffa on the north, are close to two hundred thousand Jews. There are no Arabs living in Tel Aviv but there are several thousand Jews (mostly natives) living in Jaffa on the borderland of Tel Aviv. When the riots broke out the Arabs first went after these Jews. They hunted them in their houses and shops and drove them down the streets with revolvers, clubs or whatever they could find. The Jews fled in the direction of Tel Aviv for safety.

Among those caught in the trap was a fine young Jew about twenty years old—a man trained in the universities of Germany. He had been gloriously saved in our mission home a month or two previously. It was a new life for him in every sense of the word—a life full of joy and many strange new things since, until his conversion, he had known nothing about a living God and of Christ who not only saves but also supernaturally guides and undertakes in our lives— a God who answers prayer.

Zef, for that was his Hebrew name, was visiting a Jewish friend in the northern quarter of Jaffa when suddenly he heard shooting and screaming and saw people running for their lives. He ran out into the street and saw the angry mob approaching. He started to run with the others, and as he ran he lifted his heart to his Saviour in fervent petition. The Arabs were now getting closer and in his desperation he did what he thought immediately afterward was the worst thing he could have done under the circumstances. He ran into an Arab store. He went through the front room of the small building and, not being stopped by anyone, passed through an open door into a back room. When he saw that he was trapped, he threw himself on his knees—this young man who only recently had learned to bow his knees before the Lord—and cried out to God for help.

In his race for life, Zef did not notice the Arab shopkeeper who was in the store and saw him running in. Nor did Zef have the least conception that God in His marvelous providence directed his feet into the shop of an Arab who was one of the handful of born-again Christians in the city of Jaffa. With his heart full of the love of Christ and with compassion for this Jewish lad, the Arab hurried to the back room to comfort him and to assure him that, though a Jew, he would not be harmed but would be given protection. How great was his surprise when he stepped into the back room and saw the young man on his knees! The Arab exclaimed, "I thought you were a Jew! Don't be afraid; I am a Christian." Then Zef cried, "Praise the Lord! I am a Hebrew Christian." What a time of rejoicing it was for both of them!

At nightfall this son of Ishmael led the saved son of Israel to safety, "for the love of Christ constraineth . . ." (II Corinthians 5:14).

CHAPTER 7

"If Thou Wilt, Thou Canst Make Me Clean"

IT was very unusual that Alya, the egg seller, failed to
appear at the mission home on Monday with her basket
of eggs. But when she was absent from church the next
Sunday, we knew that something was wrong, and Brother
Elias, our Arabic pastor, and I decided that we would visit
her in her village about five miles north of the city of Jerusalem. The car took us within half a mile of our destination.
From the highway which leads over the crest of the hill we de-
scended the ragged, rocky camel trail to the village in the
valley below.

Alya's small humble room was filled with neighbors, some
busying themselves around the house but most of them
crowding by her bedside and making the atmosphere rather
stifling. All indications were that Alya was very sick. It
is the custom of the women of the village to crowd around
the sick in this manner when they do not expect them to
live very long.

Alya was failing fast but she recognized us. With a big smile she reached out her arms and beckoned us to come nearer. Had we not known her for years we would have been frightened at the sight of her bare arms and hands, for they evidently were those of a leper. All the fingers were wasted away, leaving nothing but two ugly stumps. Was she dying of leprosy? No, indeed! Forty-two years ago she had been wonderfully healed of an advanced stage of leprosy and the disease had never returned. She was dying of old age, hastened by a stroke and pneumonia. Not only had Alya been healed of her leprosy but she had also been gloriously saved. But you will want to hear her own testimony. We took it down in Arabic as she gave it to us.

"I was born in a small Moslem village on the outskirts of Jerusalem and raised in a poor Moslem home. I was still a very small girl when my parents began to send me out to the fields with a flock of sheep. One day when I was about twelve years old and was alone in the fields, I saw a shepherd boy in the distance. When he saw me he came toward me. I was afraid. When he saw that I was alone he came to assault me. I screamed and the boy was frightened and ran away. I was in awful fear for sometime.

"Three or four months after this experience I noticed that I was beginning to lose control of my hands and feet as though they were paralyzed. Soon signs of leprosy appeared and the people of the village knew that I was a leper. They pronounced me unclean and drove me out of the village. I came to another village outside of the East wall of Jerusalem where there was a group of lepers. I was put among them. There I lived five terrible years. Leprosy began to eat into my flesh and bones and gradually my fingers and my toes

dropped off. One day the members of the colony decided that they would marry me to one of the men who also was a leper. I felt that it was wrong to do that and so I refused. When they could not persuade me, they beat me and put me in stocks.

"My brother, who was a Moslem priest, used to visit me. One day he told me about one of the prophets of old, called Isa [Jesus] who in His day used to perform many miracles and healed many lepers. [The Moslems, according to the teaching of the Koran, believe that Jesus was a great miracle-working prophet, but that He was succeeded and superseded by Mohammed, the greatest of all the prophets.] My brother said, 'I wish that Isa could be here. He would have compassion on you and heal you.' After this I always longed that Isa could live now and help me.

"I was still lying in the stocks because of my refusal to marry that leper when an American lady came with an interpreter. When she saw me in my plight she asked me why I was treated this way. I told her. She asked me, 'Do you believe that Christ can heal you?' Then she told me the wonderful story of the Saviour who can save and heal. She told me that she wanted to take me to her home if I was willing. They let me go and I went to live with her in Jerusalem. She gave me some black medicine. Then she and another lady prayed for me. I continued to take that medicine. After three months an American doctor came to us. The lady asked him to examine me. He took some of my blood and went away. A few months later, after his arrival in America, he wrote that they examined my blood and that I had no trace of leprosy left. I was healed!

"Oh, what a wonderful feeling it was after more than five years of awful suffering. I know that the medicine could not have effected the healing in such a short time. It was the Lord Jesus Christ Himself. When I first was taken into the home I promised the lady that if I were healed I would accept the Lord Jesus as my Saviour.

"It has been now about forty years since the Lord healed me and saved me. I am still living in my native village testifying to the power of Christ. I am making my living now buying up the eggs of my village and bringing them into Jerusalem on my donkey for sale to the dear missionaries. And of course every Sunday I come in on my donkey to the Alliance Church."

Alya was a unique character and known all over the city of Jerusalem. She collected eggs in her village and rode her donkey to the city every Monday. Though her two feet were only two stumps like her hands, she learned to walk on them and handled herself, the donkey and the basket of eggs very well.

She would bring her basket into the house and squat beside it, while Mrs. Freed counted out the eggs, so many for a quarter. Alya had a small cloth bag around her neck, like a necklace to hold her money. When we paid for the eggs we put the money in the bag for her and made the change if necessary. After the business transaction, Alya never failed to request a short Bible study and prayer. We three would have a lovely time of fellowship around the Word. She always prayed last, remembering all the Alliance missionaries who ministered to her in Jerusalem, beginning with those who prayed for her as a leper girl, and on down the list to us. She earnestly pleaded for souls and for revival. When she finished her prayer and while still on her knees she would invariably pronounce the benediction.

As we stood by the bedside of this dear old faithful woman our hearts were filled with praises to the Lord. She must have felt what was in our hearts because suddenly, with her eyes closed, she began to sing the chorus of that old familiar hymn, beautifully rendered in the Arabic:

> In the Cross, in the Cross,
>   Be my glory ever;
> Till my raptured soul shall find
>   Rest beyond the river.

The room was filled with bigoted Moslem men and women who listened respectfully while zealous Brother Elias took advantage of the opportunity and explained the meaning of the words of the hymn—a kind of indirect preaching.

A few days later Alya, the leper doubly cleansed, went to her heavenly reward.

CHAPTER 8

"I Have Set Before Thee an Open Door"

YOU will go to my native village very soon and tell my people of the Saviour and this wonderful salvation, won't you?"

Gideon was full of enthusiasm as he urged me, his father in the faith, to take the Gospel story to the village of Jebaib, hidden in the interior of the Druze Mountains of Syria. Up to that time this region was one of the most neglected parts of that land beyond the Jordan.

We had been looking to the Lord daily for another new open door. Short visits are possible to most of the Arab villages but repeated visits and extended ministries are only possible as the Lord gives us friends and open hearts in a

49

village. Gideon's recent conversion, through Mr. Brooks, in
Dera'a, the main station of that area, and his longing to
bring the message of salvation to his own people, meant such
an open door and of course we eagerly entered it.

On our first visit to Jebaib we took Gideon with us. He
led us right to his home where his widowed mother lived
and after giving us a taste of simple but generous Arab
hospitality he started out to bring in some of his intimate
friends. Before long several young men were sitting around
listening to the story of the Gospel.

Gideon and his friends were of the Oriental Orthodox
(Catholic) faith. Though this sect has never owed allegiance
to Rome, yet they have throughout the centuries adapted
most of its idolatrous and false doctrines. Their priests,
apart from the natural temptations which their office and
hold on the people would present, are doubly corrupt because
their church does not possess the riches of Rome. Consequently the priests depend on their own trickery and graft
to squeeze material things out of these poor people. This
foul business seems to be the priests' only aim in life. These
people live in the midst of overwhelmingly Moslem communities, and while boasting of their form of "Christianity,"
they are steeped in superstition, sin and moral degradation
equal to that of their Moslem fellow villagers. Protestantism
is an anathema to them. Fortunately, from their viewpoint, it
has not yet "defiled" many of their villages.

There was something in Gideon's testimony, never heard
in his village before, that made these young men think. We
left the village after placing the Word of God in the hands
of one or two who could read.

Three hundred Arab villages—for which we alone were
responsible—were challenging us. Thus many weeks passed

before we found another opportunity to visit Jebaib again. When we made our second visit, we found several of the young men eager to listen. Among them was Mutlak, a bright young man about twenty years old. He could read fluently, an unusual achievement in those primitive villages, and was keen to grasp the truth. He had been diligently, though secretly, studying the Arabic New Testament which we had left with him on our previous visit and his heart was hungry and prepared by the Holy Spirit. He insisted that we have a gathering in his home. His father and brothers were out in the field plowing and would not get back home until sunset, so we could meet unmolested, since of course the women did not count anyhow.

Mutlak did not realize, however, that his uncle, who was the priest of the village, had already been informed that his own nephew was becoming interested in the accursed doctrines of the missionary. When we arrived in the village he secretly followed us and while we were gathering in Mutlak's house with several young men hungry for the Word, suddenly the priest rushed in, and enraged started to shout and curse at us. He grabbed the young men and one by one threw them out of the room, and while he was thus engaged he was heaping his vile condemnation upon us as the source of all this trouble which had been brought to their village. After he pushed Mutlak out of the door he came right toward me, hatred literally gleaming in his eyes, but as he raised his hands he suddenly dropped them again and rushed out of the room.

By this time a large group of people had gathered and he began to shout at the top of his voice and denounce me and the damnable Protestant religion which brings nothing but trouble, strife and misery in its wake. However, when he realized that no one was opposing him and that he could not stir up an argument or a fight with the missionary, he gradually quieted down and left the place.

Soon the young men returned to the room and looked at me in great amazement. They had never seen strife end in this way before. As I found out afterwards it was right then and there that Mutlak, who had already fully understood God's plan of salvation, gave his heart to the Lord Jesus Christ and decided to follow this despised way. After we offered a short but fervent prayer to God and committed these young hungry hearts into His protecting hands we left the village.

When we returned to Jebaib several weeks later we found Mutlak saved and rejoicing in the Lord. Moreover, he introduced us to a friend of his whom he had led to the Lord in the meantime. This young man was Ibrahim, the keeper of the only store (if one may give it such an exalted name) in the village. Later Ibrahim went through great suffering for his Lord and was a "corn of wheat" who had brought forth fruit in his village and elsewhere to the glory of his Saviour.

CHAPTER 9

"Except a Corn of Wheat..."

BEFORE many weeks had passed Mutlak's father realized that the new-found faith was not a mere passing fancy but a deep-seated conviction in the heart of his son. The father, stirred up by his brother, the priest, and feeling the shame and disgrace that had come to his home, gave Mutlak a final warning to get the foolishness out of his head or else he would have to leave his home with his wife and baby. Here in America this might not mean much beyond the sorrow of separation, but in Arabia it means everything.

The Arab village farmers live a kind of communal and tribal life. The aged father possesses the land and the home, and his children even after marriage live with him and work for him in full and unquestioned obedience to his will.

They do not live on the farm but in the village which is surrounded in every direction by the land owned by them. In their miserable little houses—dark and dingy and usually consisting of only one or two rooms—they crowd in the ever growing family. The father supplies food, shelter and clothing for his sons and their families and in return the men work on the land. They leave the village daily and in some cases travel one or even two hours by foot or on donkeyback to reach their field. Yet with all the poverty and misery it is home to them and they are well satisfied.

Mutlak counted the cost and told his father that he could not deny his new found faith. The father was enraged and put him out of the house with his wife and child, and left them on the street with nothing but a few pieces of old dirty bedding. There was only one thing Mutlak, or anyone in his position, could do. In every village there are usually a few families who possess more land than they are able to cultivate and so are in need of hired help. Mutlak found such a family and offered his services. This does not sound bad to us; however, in the Orient it is often almost like being sold into slavery.

Mutlak and his little family now lived a bitter life of drudgery. They were given the poorest place in the house for living quarters—a corner of a dark room next to the goats and donkey. Their diet consisted of not much more than plain barley bread, while at home they often enjoyed wheat bread with such extras as olives, olive oil, raisin-molasses and even occasional mutton for feasting. Now Mutlak had to do the hardest work in the field with no privileges whatsoever.

One day I went to visit a few believers and friends in the village, and planned to go out to the field where Mutlak worked to comfort him in his sorrow and suffering. To my surprise and joy he greeted me with a radiant smile and told me how happy he was in the Lord and that he was praying that the Lord would use his life of willing obedience to His glory and to the salvation of souls. How abundantly God honored and answered his self-sacrificing desire we shall see later.

Such victories as we began to see in the village of Jebaib could not be unnoticed and unchallenged by Satan. The life and testimony of these few but earnest believers were becoming a thorn in the flesh and a living rebuke to their fellow villagers. Lying, stealing, deception, hatred, blood feuds, bitter revenge and similar evils are the order of the day in these Arab villages. Now light had come in the midst of darkness; truthfulness, honesty in dealings with their fellow men and the government, love, kindness, the spirit of forgiveness in the lives of the believers—these were too conspicuous, and indeed made the people of the village uncomfortable. True is the Word and in a very real sense evident in the lands of the East to this very day: "And this is the condemnation, that light is come into the world, and men loved darkness rather than light, because their deeds were evil. For every one that doeth evil hateth the light, neither cometh to the light, lest his deeds should be reproved."

Wicked men of the village sent word to the French Governor of the province that the American missionaries were using religious prejudices to stir up strife among the "peaceful" population of the village. The Governor had no right to forbid us to preach but he sent instructions through one of his officers to the elders of the village that the people dare not have any dealings with us, otherwise they would be punished.

Soon after these instructions were issued it was time for another visit to Jebaib. We were absolutely ignorant of what had taken place since our last visit and were looking forward to a good time of ministry to the believers as well as to others who were becoming very friendly to us. Brother Barnaba—our faithful native evangelist—accompanied me and when we arrived in the village we started toward the home of one of the believers. We soon noticed a strange coldness on the part of the peple whom we passed. Next I noticed one of the friendliest men of the village coming toward us but suddenly he turned away and started in the other direction. We were puzzled. We arrived now at our destination and found Ibrahim, one of the believers whom Mutlak had led to the Lord, in the house. Without taking time for the otherwise profuse and indispensable exchange of greetings, Ibrahim, with a very serious look on his face, said to me, "Brother Freed, I would urge you to leave the village right away." Then he explained that the Governor had ordered the people of the village not to have any dealings with us, and that they were therefore stirred up against the missionaries and against the believers.

I realized, though not fully, the seriousness of the situation and suggested to Ibrahim that we have prayer together. We got on our knees and one of us had just begun to pray when suddenly somebody dashed into the room. We all stood up and faced the mukhtar (the chief) of the village. Shouting at the top of his voice he said: "Mr. Freed, I advise you to leave the village immediately, otherwise there will be bloodshed." I turned to Ibrahim and Brother Barnaba and requested them to keep calm and quiet. Then we stepped outdoors and faced a mob of fifty or sixty men, both young and old. At that moment Mutlak, who had also

heard of my arrival, stepped up to me bravely and greeted me
very warmly. I quickly told him to keep sweet and
silent, for I realized that our believers were in even greater
danger than we were. By this time some of the young men
started to throw stones at us. With only a word of farewell
to Mutlak and Ibrahim, we walked past the mob and left
the village.

We returned home to Dera's, our main station, quite
discouraged. The Lord had wonderfully opened the doors of
Jebaib and worked in hearts far beyond our expectation. It
had seemed that the village would become one of our most
fruitful out-stations, and in an unusually short time, but now
the doors of Jebaib were suddenly slammed in our faces.

The weeks and months that followed often found us, as
we itinerated in the district, with our hearts lifted up in
fervent prayer for the reopening of Jebaib and the protection of the believers. Six months passed before the answer
came.

The French Governor who had issued the edict against us
went to France for his annual summer furlough. He left
everything behind, for he fully expected to return and re-
sume his office. However, for some reason which we never
found out, he was not permitted to return to the Near East.
Instructions were sent from France to have all his belongings
shipped to him. No one in Soueida, the capital of the Druze
Domain where his headquarters were, could understand such
a strange procedure. We could—God answered prayer!

Soon word was sent to us by friends in Jebaib to come
and visit them. It was a happy day when we again entered
the village, not only to find our believers as we left them
but to hear the triumphant sequel to Mutlak's story of
suffering.

One day while Mutlak was working out in the field he noticed an old man coming toward him. The man looked like his own father, but Mutlak quickly dismissed that thought. His father's land lay on the other side of the village, and besides it was inconceivable that the old man would have anything to do with him. Yet it was his father who came right up to him and said, "Son, ever since you left me I have been unhappy. You have been my best and most faithful son and I cannot live without you. Won't you come back home?"

Now to have an Arab father approach his son in this manner for reconciliation was nothing short of a miracle. It was a great test to Mutlak. Surely he longed to be back home with his little family where they could have at least a measure of comfort and proper food and where he could be delivered from his present toil and misery. But the love of Christ his Saviour was brightly burning in his soul and he was not willing to return home at the cost of denying his Lord. He looked in the face of his father and said. "Father, you know that I love you and I long to come home, but I am willing to return only if I may remain true to my newly found faith."

The reply was a blow to the father who thought that if he humbled himself to the extent of coming to his son and asking him to come home, Mutlak would surely be glad and willing to forget his foolish ideas. There was a struggle within but finally the father's love conquered. "All right, come home," he said in resignation.

This is the story Mutlak told me when I visited the village after six months of forced absence. He invited me to his father's house. On the way we passed his uncle, the priest, who was sitting in front of his house. I cordially greeted him; he gave me a terrible look, then in a curt manner returned the greeting. I found Mutlak's father friendly and I spent a happy hour there, my heart overflowing with praise.

Another six months passed which brought about, through the life and testimony of Mutlak, a great change in his father and all of his family. Their home, from which Mutlak had once been literally driven, became the regular place for the believers to gather for worship and fellowship. Several members of Mutlak's family became true followers of the Lord Jesus Christ and the Lord sent a gracious revival to the village.

Still another year passed and we celebrated the dedication of a little chapel built with the sacrificial gifts and labors of our believers in Jebaib together with those of others. Mutlak, of course, was there rejoicing in the goodness of the Lord and in the faithfulness of our God.

God abundantly fulfilled in the life of Mutlak, this simple Arab boy, His own Word and promise, "Except a corn of wheat fall into the ground and die, it abideth alone: *but if it die*, it bringeth forth much fruit" (John 12:24).

CHAPTER 10

"His Ways Past Finding Out!"

WE were journeying from Jerusalem to Haifa at a time when travel was hazardous in Palestine. Risks from violence within and without made one think twice before venturing too far from home. However, our call was urgent and challenging. Several of our Arab believers in Haifa were anxious to be baptized. We stayed overnight in a Jewish colony instead of going through to Haifa, although the trip could have been easily made in one day.

Late in the afternoon we heard the sirens of the air-raid alarm, that unforgettable sound. We ran for the shelter—the basement of the pension—and could hear the roaring of the planes overhead. Later on we learned about the

double attacks of the Italian raiders. They first visited
Haifa, the place where we were planning to have our baptismal service, and dropped their bombs on oil tanks. Then
they flew to Tel Aviv, passing over the colony where we
were, and bombed the heart of the residential section of
that city.

The next day we arrived in Haifa. With the hope that
the bombing would not be repeated, we proceeded with the
baptismal service. It was a blessed service on the shores
of the Mediterranean Sea. Back of each baptism was a story
of God's wonder-working power in the lives of these humble
people. But of those present none had a more wonderful
story to tell than a young Arab couple who had been married
only a few months before. They could testify, as they thought
of God's providential leadings in their lives, that indeed
His ways are "past finding out." This is the story.

Hanna and Farha were both brought up in the village of
Tisia in Hauran, Syria. According to the age-old Arab
custom, they were chosen by their parents for each other.
As is the usual way, the two fathers made the bargain while
the children were small.

When Hanna became old enough to work he was expected
to begin payments on the price set for the girl. Being an
ambitious young man he was not satisfied with the life of
drudgery which these village farmers had to lead. He left
for the city, went to school for a short time and soon found
work as teacher in a village school. It was in this village,
a long way from his own, where the Lord opened the way for
us to preach the Gospel that Hanna was among those saved.

In the meantime Hanna heard of the opportunities in
the great city of Haifa, in Palestine, and, traveling a great
part of the journey on foot, he finally reached Haifa.

Soon he came in contact with our Alliance Church in that city, and under the devoted ministry of our evangelist and pastor, Brother Abdullah, Hanna grew steadily in the grace and knowledge of our Lord.

For more than a year Hanna had been faithfully sending money home to his village in payment of his obligation to his prospective father-in-law. He expected that in one more year he would have completed the payments and would be ready to marry the girl. But now the Lord began to speak to him about his proposed marriage to Farha, who was unsaved.

On the occasion of one of my visits to the church in Haifa, Hanna opened his heart to me. I was deeply impressed by his earnestness and desire to do the will of God, though to me his proposal seemed rather unusual. He told me that the Lord had been speaking to him about the wrong of marrying an unbeliever. "I am willing right now, Brother Freed, to give up the girl and lose the money I have already paid," he said, "but somehow the Lord seems to tell me not to do that but to pray for Farha's salvation." I told him that I believed he should pray for her salvation, provided he was determined in his heart not to marry her until the Lord answered his prayer. Hanna promised to continue to pray for the girl, and, with a request that I support him in faith, we parted.

Months passed before my next visit to Haifa. At the gathering of the believers Hanna met me with a glowing countenance; he was waving a letter in his hand. "Brother Freed, the Lord answered prayer," he fairly shouted to me. The letter was from Farha's brother who lived in the village of Edder in Transjordan and it told a wonderful story.

While Hanna was in Haifa, Farha in her village began to lose her health. As time went on her condition became worse and worse. Finally, just about the time we started to pray with Hanna for the Lord to save Farha, and unknown to him, Farha's parents decided to send her to her married brother in Transjordan. They hoped that the change of climate and surroundings might be beneficial to her. It was not a simple matter to send her on the long journey, but everything worked out favorably and she reached her brother's home.

Farha found a great change in her brother. At first she did not understand it but as the weeks went by she was deeply impressed by his life. Of course, the secret was that Farha's brother, through the ministries of our missionary and native worker living in Kerak, Transjordan, had been saved sometime before Farha's visit. His life and testimony reached her heart.

Soon after Farha's conversion she began to think of her fiancé, Hanna, and became concerned about his spiritual welfare. The brother and sister decided that they would write to Hanna on her behalf (she did not know how to write), giving their testimony and urging him to give his heart to the Lord. It was this letter that had reached Hanna shortly before my second visit. When I read it I could understand his excitement and joy. The Lord had answered his prayers in a wonderful way. One could imagine the rejoicing in that humble home in the village of Edder when the brother and sister received the news that Hanna had already been saved.

A few months later there was a wedding at the mission compound in Kerak, the missionary, Mr. Ward, uniting Hanna and Farha in truly holy matrimony. And when at the baptismal service in Haifa this young Arab couple gave their testimony and followed the Lord in the waters of baptism, the joy and gratitude of the believers who witnessed the scene knew no bounds. What an example of co-ordination, through divine providence, of our work in Palestine, Transjordan and Syria. Truly "his ways [are] past finding out" (Romans 11:33).

CHAPTER 11

"Men Loved Darkness Rather Than Light"

THE two stories related in this chapter fit together well because of the similarity and the contrast which they present. The stories are about two boys who lived in different villages. They both ran away from home as the result of the preaching of the Gospel, but their motives were different.

In John 3:20,21 we read: "For every one that doeth evil hateth the light, neither cometh to the light, lest his deeds should be reproved. But he that doeth truth cometh to the light, that his deeds may be made manifest, that they are wrought in God." The two boys ran away from home but the one ran away from the light and the other ran to the light. It makes a great difference which way we run.

* * *

Obed lived in the town of Dera'a and had a reputation even among those untrained, spoiled Arab children of being a very wicked boy. His mother tried in vain to bring him under control. One day she heard that the "Americans" (the American missionaries and native workers) had a class for boys where those who attended were strangely changed for the better. So she decided to try it, not because she had any interest or sympathy for the Gospel but because she hoped that it might work magic for her child.

Our faithful native evangelist, David, held this Bible class for boys in Dera'a on Fridays—the day the Moslem children do not attend school. Obed joined the class which consisted of about fifteen children around twelve to four-teen years of age.

However, the wicked heart of Obed rebelled against the teaching of the Gospel and gradually his hatred centered on David himself. And so Obed conceived a scheme to do David harm.

One day when Obed came home from the Bible class he said to his mother, "Mother, do you know what David told me today? David told me that if I let him make me a Chris-tian, he will send me to the far-away great city of Jerusalem, will put me in an American school, put on me clothes just like they wear and besides all that will give me two hundred dollars." The mother, knowing her boy, did not believe a word of the story.

Next day the boy went to school. Afternoon came and the time for Obed to return but he did not come home. Sup-per time came but he did not make his appearance. The mother inquired in the neighborhood and learned that people had seen him in the morning but not since. Bedtime came but no sign of Obed. His mother spent an anxious and wake-

ful night. The morning light broke and still the boy had
not come home. By this time the mother came to the conclusion that Obed must have told the truth—perhaps for the
first time in his life. · Yes, that man David who worked for
the Americans must have kidnaped him. She reported it
to the police. They were only too eager to find an excuse to
do us harm and so they came, took dear David and marched
him off to prison.

It was in January, the middle of the cold rainy season.
They put David in a large room with absolutely no furniture.
It had three bare walls, open iron bars on the fourth side
and cold cement floors. Here David was placed with about
twenty-five others, all hardened criminals. He was given
only one blanket. The following day I took some blankets
to the prison and asked the guard to give them to David, but
he gruffly refused. "All prisoners are treated alike," he said.

We appealed to the highest native officials but received
the cynical answer, "Prove to us that David did not kidnap
the boy and we will release him." We appealed to the French
authorities but they told us that since David was a native
they could not interfere in the matter. Then they gave me
this comforting assurance, "You are fortunate that you are
an American citizen, otherwise you might be in prison, too."

Much prayer went up to the throne of grace on David's
behalf. Days passed and the cold and exposure to which
David was not accustomed were having their effect. First
he had a bad cold, then fever and we feared it was develop-
ing into pneumonia. During all that time, however, David
was faithfully witnessing to his fellow prisoners.

Finally at the end of two weeks we received the joyful
report that Obed was back in the village. He confessed
to the officials that he had long been desirous of leaving

home and going to the city of Damascus as an adventure, for
he pictured the wonderful and luxurious life he would live
there. In order to cover up his escape and only too glad to
do David harm for telling him about Jesus, he had invented
the story of David's offer to send him to Jerusalem. When
he reached Damascus he did not find it as easy to make
a living as he had thought. In fact he walked the streets
of that great heartless city and begged and stole food. Finally, cold, hungry and homesick he had returned home, sub-
dued but not at all repentant.

It was a happy day when I was notified that I could come
and take David out of prison. The poor man could hardly
stand on his feet and so with his arm around my shoulder
and neck we made our way slowly home.

You will undoubtedly wonder just what the Lord did
work out through this testing. Sometimes we can clearly
follow the Lord's hand and see how He turns testings
and sufferings to blessings and to the salvation of souls.
We shall relate such incidents in subsequent chapters.
Often the Lord would simply ask us to accept such testings
as some of the "all things" that "work together for good,"
and to rest assured that the testimony both in word and in
deed will bear fruit.

* * *

Thani was a boy who was also about thirteen years of age.
He lived in a small village in the Druze Mountain district.
A large part of the population of this village were Orthodox
and Catholic Arabs. In spite of the fanaticism of the people
and their hostility toward the Gospel, we found a sufficient
number of those who were friendly to make it possible for us
to come to the village of Jebaib for two weeks of ministries.

All day long groups, small and large, would visit us in the dark, dingy room which had been placed at our disposal by a friend. Some were brought there by curiosity and others by real interest.

Thani dropped in every time he had a chance when he thought that his people would not know about it. He loved to hear and learn Gospel choruses. More than once this poor boy was found out by his family and this invariably resulted in a terrible beating for him. But his heart was being drawn to the Lord whose Name until now he had mainly used in connection with an oath or curse.

The Lord graciously worked in these meetings but at the end of two weeks we had to leave. Several months later Mrs. Freed and I were at our mission home at the main station in Dera'a. One day we heard a knock on the door and when we opened it we saw little Thani standing there with a guilty yet pleading look on his face. "Mr. Freed," he said, "I'll work for you if you let me stay with you. I want to hear more about Jesus." We questioned him and found out that he had run away from home because his heart was hungry. What a difference between the running away of the two boys, Obed and Thani! We could well make use of Thani's help on the mission compound. We realized that his parents would not care. In most of the villages these boys do not attend school at all and are needed by their parents only during harvest time. Otherwise each child is regarded as a burden and a hungry mouth to feed. So we agreed to keep Thani and of course notified his parents.

We fixed him a cot, the first he had ever slept on, since in his village they all sleep on the floor. Our food was simply luxurious compared with the plain barley bread which had been his main dish at home.

Every morning Thani joined us in our family worship and how he enjoyed the Gospel stories and the songs we taught him! He learned to know and love our son Paul who was at home at this time for his vacation from school in Beirut.

One day Mrs. Freed called Thani but received no response. When she went out into the kitchen to see what he was doing she found him in a corner with a piece of mirror set on the shelf before him and scissors in his hand. You may not know that the village Arabs all let their hair grow in long locks and a good many have them braided. You do not often see this in pictures because they always wear a shawl-like headgear which covers their hair. "What in the world are you doing, Thani?" exclaimed Mrs. Freed. Thani looking very guilty and with tears in his eyes muttered, "I want to look like Paul." He was cutting off his long locks and giving himself an "American" haircut!

But dear Thani not only wanted to look like Paul he wanted Paul's Saviour to be his Saviour, too.

Then one day he came to me and said, "You have been so kind to me but I feel that I should go back to my people and tell them about Jesus." And so he went away from our home and left behind comforts and loving friends to return to a life of poverty, misery and hatred that he might bear testimony to the power of Christ to save a small Arab boy.

"But he that doeth truth cometh to the light, that his deeds may be made manifest, that they are wrought in God."

CHAPTER 12

"But Joy Cometh in the Morning"

THE task of reaching the many Arab villages with so few helpers is overwhelming. To try to figure out from the human viewpoint which village to evangelize and which to neglect would be futile. It is blessed to realize amid such perplexities the faithful leading of the Holy Spirit, who goes before and prepares the way. The Lord taught us that opening these communities for the Gospel requires grace and perseverance. It is wonderful to see that when He leads He will turn apparent defeat into victory and heartaches and weeping into rejoicing.

We were particularly burdened for a certain village. Though we had made several short visits there some months apart, we saw no outward result but only resentment toward our message. However, the Lord gave us a friend who urged us to come back again and stay in his home for a longer period. We felt that the Lord was opening the door.

It was not a simple task to bring our car, loaded inside, on the running boards and the back right to the top, into the village and within the courtyard of a friend. We spent several hours on the way, crossing open fields and moving stones to make a path for travel. Now in the village we had to move more stones. The narrow crooked lanes were not planned for automobiles but for donkeys and camels. When our more modern car with its low wheel base and large fenders gets caught in stepping-stones laid across the streets or hooked in corner stones and curbstones and stone posts, it would be a pleasure to go back to our dear old Model T if only it had a new engine or a pair of wings. The last act before reaching our destination was to tear down the entrance into the courtyard. This, however, was not as serious as it sounds because the entrance was made of only two huge pieces of stones too close to each other to admit a car. We rebuilt it again when we left the village at the end of our stay.

Our friend welcomed us into his humble home. It consisted of a long room divided into two parts by a thin, mud-plastered bamboo partition. This reached high enough to obstruct the view from one section into the other but not high enough to keep out the sound. We could hear mumblings and groanings which came from beyond the partition. We were informed that the occupant was a dear old woman, a great-aunt of our host; he said she would not disturb us, but this was not the case.

It always takes some minutes before the eye becomes adjusted to these simple village homes. You enter from the glaring sunshine, which for ten months out of twelve is never softened or dimmed by a cloud, into a room without any windows. Light and air comes in only through the door when it is left open. However, apart from the people there is very little to see. Almost the first item of equipment or furniture you will discover is a stack of bedding. Part of his bedding is white (or at least it once was white) and part consists of brightly colored mats, quilts, covers and pillows. They immediately attract the eye of the newcomer to the corner of the room where they are folded and stacked during the day.

Our host, who was rather prosperous according to their standards, also possessed a crudely made wooden box which was the size of a small trunk and brightly painted. This is the treasure chest and contains the family's "Sunday garments," two or three cheap pieces of crockery such as a saucer, a cup and perhaps a plate kept for distinguished guests, also a tin spoon or two. The family jewelry, a towel, a bar of perfumed soap and a few trinkets complete the contents of the box. It is always kept under lock and key, and the key is never trusted to anyone except the male head of the family. If he has ever been away from his village to the city and is rather well to do, you might be surprised to see such luxuries as a flashlight, a mouth organ or even an alarm clock carefully guarded inside the locked box. A round mat hangs on the wall and is placed on the floor at mealtime to serve as a table. This, with a small coal-oil lamp, completes the furnishings.

Our good friend planned to vacate the room for us for the period of our stay. It was a simple operation. He and his wife grabbed part of the bedding, threw it over their heads and walked off to the neighbors where they were to stay. In these humble homes one can learn real hospitality, whole-heartedly given. They have very little to offer either in space or things but such as they have is given gladly and without any restriction or hesitation. Our friend simply told the neighbor, "We are coming to stay with you for a few days," and the immediate reply was *ahlan wa sahlan*—a welcome really meant. In these homes there is always room for more. They simply crowd a little closer together. They sleep with hardly any of their clothing removed, men, women and children all in a row. If the cover is not wide enough, it is turned around lengthwise, thus leaving their feet sticking out. It seems that the Arab is never cold if his head and face are covered. You see them in the cold rainy winter, wading through the wet muddy fields barefooted but with their faces well wrapped.

Our missionary party consisted of three—a native evangelist, a missionary colleague and myself. We brought in our cots and bedding, a portable kerosene cookstove, a few utensils and some staple foods. To carry such elaborate equipment with us in itinerary evangelistic work among the Arabs is not the regular but the exceptional thing. It can be done only when we have become well known and have found a special friend who is willing to place his house at our disposal. Otherwise we must enter the village without bedding and without food and are expected to accept the hospitality of the people, which means eating their food and sleeping with them on their bedding. Normally it would be the greatest insult to them if we brought our supplies with us. It means to them only one thing—that we reject their hospitality.

We spent our first evening in making personal calls of respect to the mukhtar or sheik and other important personages. Then we retired. Soon we found out, as we invariably do, that when our host vacated the room for us, he did not do a thorough job. Flees and creeping things of all kinds abounded in the room. Mice, chewing on the straw mixed in the mud plaster of the walls, kept us company. Our good brother, the evangelist, insisted that he heard a snake all night in a sack of grain.

Throughout the day we made many contacts and announced a meeting in our room for the evening. The people came crowding into the room and sat on the floor. We are happy to have this first opportunity for a public meeting. We started to teach them some simple choruses, when a frightful noise coming from the adjoining room interrupted us. We found out later that a group of young men, eighteen to twenty years of age, had banded together to break up our meeting. They entered the room where the dear old woman lived, pushed her out and took possession of the place. When we started the singing, they started the chanting of filthy, immoral songs. We lifted our hearts in prayer to the Lord that He would stop them, but they carried on. We tried to read the Word but could hardly hear. We tried singing again but to no avail. They persisted. Finally there was nothing left to do but to dismiss the meeting. We did that with heavy hearts, and the people left.

We felt discouraged. It is so difficult to find an opening in these Arab villages and it takes months of preparation and prayer before we can reach the stage when, as in this village, we are able to stay for a period and conduct meetings. The Lord certainly helped us thus far, but now Satan seemed to have the victory. The next day we knew it would be worse. We spent a long time praying and planning and it was after midnight when, with heavy hearts, we retired. It was truly a night of weeping.

About daybreak there was a knock on our door. I opened it and there stood a young man. "Please forgive me for disturbing you so early," he said in a very apologetic manner, "but I could not wait any longer. I want to speak with you." He came in and sat down on the floor in the customary manner. "You don't know me," he started his story, "but I am one of those young men who were in the next room last evening. In fact I am the leader of that gang. We banded together determined to break up your meeting and to make it impossible for you to carry on in our village. When I saw how successful we were in our first effort and that you had to discontinue the meeting, I felt very happy and proud. I went home feeling mighty good about my success. But when I retired for the night I could not sleep. The more I thought about it, the worse I felt, until I realized what a mean, wicked thing I did in fighting against God. I could hardly wait for daybreak to come to ask your forgiveness for what I have done." We gladly forgave him and he left.

That evening we had another gathering in our room, but it was different from the one the evening before. The adjoining room was quiet and empty, but with us and sitting as close to the speaker as he could get, was Ghattas, the leader of the band of boys. Several of his accomplices were with him—all listening to the message and learning about the Lord Jesus Christ. A few days later Ghattas was wonderfully saved and was the first fruit of a gracious working of the Lord in that village in the months that followed. "Weeping may endure for a night, but joy cometh in the morning" (Psalm 30:6).

CHAPTER 13*

"Beauty for Ashes"

S OME years ago when we were on our way from Palestine for our furlough, we stopped at London for several days and were privileged one morning to see the brilliant and magnificent crown jewels of England displayed in London Tower. Among them is the Black Prince ruby, a gem about the size of a hen's egg. How gorgeous! How costly! What could be more beautiful than this ruby? One might quickly answer: Queen Victoria, who first wore it in her crown.

How true is Proverbs 31:10, "Who can find a virtuous woman? for her price is far above rubies"! But what a con-

* This chapter was contributed by my wife and companion in the labors of the Gospel.

trast the queen's life and environment were to those of the poor village women of the Near East!

Poverty, ignorance and fatalism all tend to make their lot a pitiable one. In home life, they are simply slaves to work; in social life, they have no recreation except snatches here and there of neighborhood gossip. The men do get together, talking, smoking and drinking their coffee in the evening hours, but the women stay at home to care for the children and to work. While in Christian lands the weaker sex is honored and preferred, it is not so in the villages of the Orient. In everything the women take what is left. If there is one donkey, the man rides; the woman walks. The man wears the shoes; the woman trudges along on the stony roads or in mud and rain, barefooted. At meals the men sit down and eat; the women serve them and the food that is left is handed to them. In spiritual things, the woman is hardly considered as having a soul.

Let me take you to a little Arab village in the ancient land of Bashan, south of Damascus, Syria, where thousands of years ago Og, king of Bashan, reigned. The land and people remain truly Oriental. The state of the people and their habits are just what they were in the days of Abraham.

The houses are built of black volcanic stone, very unattractive, and water is scarce. All around there is not a blade of grass or a shrub or a tree in sight—nothing but black stones everywhere on the bare plateau as far as one can see. The people are fearfully poor, and dirty because water is so scarce. But as we lived among them, we found them kind-hearted and lovable.

In this village lived one of God's jewels, a poor Christian Arab woman who out of her poverty found something to do for the Lord Jesus. Our natural minds cannot conceive how jewels can be gathered in a place where such sin, poverty and ignorance abound—but God is able!

Let me give you a glimpse into this woman's life. Her house consists of one room with walls from three to four feet thick, built of blocks of black stones roughly dressed and laid in mud plaster. When one enters the door of the room, he finds that about two-thirds of the space is a slightly raised platform. This platform is occupied by the family while the lower part is used for the donkey and goats. A small hole through the wall furnishes the only entrance for a little light and at the same time serves as an exit for the smoke which on winter days fairly fills the house.

Long before sunrise this Arab woman is up to make bread and to do the countless other duties which fall to her share before it is time to start out in the fields for harvesting, or to grind the corn for the day's consumption, or to go to the public pool and carry a heavy load of water on her head, up the hill, back to the village. The life of these peasant women is terribly hard and dreary, and it is no wonder that they are old at an age when their Western sisters have scarcely come to their prime.

In this village a few years ago we built a little church for a group of Arab Christians, and each believer did his share in helping to put up the building. Some dug or cut stones, and lent their camels or donkeys to carry the stone from the quarries or to transport various materials; others carried water, and mixed mud, water and straw for plastering, with their feet.

Among the believers was an old woman, poor, ignorant, unable to read or write. She asked, "What can I do to help? My husband is not saved, and I have nothing of my own to contribute." We told her that the Lord surely would take good intentions for the deed in her case, but she was not satisfied. She did not rest until she found out that they were in great need of ashes for the mortar since sand was very difficult to obtain.

So bright and early each morning, with a sweet radiant smile upon her old wrinkled face, she would go to her neighbors and urge them not to dump out their ashes but to let her collect them. Many hours during the day she could be seen going back and forth between the homes and the church building with a basket of ashes on her head; she was carrying them joyfully for her Lord.

Soon the little church was completed. It stands on the outskirts of the village, and there Christian Arab men and women with their children gather several times a week to worship God. There they bring in others, and lead them to a knowledge of saving grace through Jesus Christ their Lord.

When the Lord makes up His jewels, this poor, ignorant woman will be included because she accepted God's Pearl of great price, the Lord Jesus Christ who redeemed her, not with corruptible things as silver and gold, but with His own precious blood.

Truly this woman had "beauty for ashes." Let us then turn our ashes into beauty these days when there are so many sad burdened hearts whom we can help.

CHAPTER 14

"Choosing Rather to Suffer..."

THE conversion of Martha caused quite a stir in her village. In these Arab communities life is laid out in a rather rigid pattern. Things in the religious as well as in the social realm conform to age-old customs which are jealously guarded by young and old, rich and poor. In fact there is no privacy in the life of these peasant farmers. Everybody knows everybody else's affairs; not only do they know them, but they feel perfectly free to interfere. The low moral and ethical standards of personal and social life are collectively approved and woe to those persons who would dare to question them or set themselves against them. In fact no one does—or rather no one did until the Lord began to work.

Darkness hates light and those who live in the darkness of sin and degradation resent the searchlight of the Gospel because it uncovers their corruption of heart. We in the United States are accustomed to high standards of morality and righteousness in personal, social and business dealings. Fairness, honesty and truthfulness are the usual thing and the opposite of them the exception. Though the majority of our people do not want Christ to rule over them, yet they have a heritage which at least approves and appreciates Christian standards. It is not so in the lands where the light of the Gospel has not penetrated for centuries. In our land no one would be persecuted for forsaking lies and turning to truthfulness or forsaking dishonesty and turning to fair dealing. But the story is different when suddenly one is born again in an Arab community where there are only a few Christians. Everything about the new life and changed actions of the child of God becomes a source of antagonism to every one.

Martha's changed life was like the waving of a red flag before a bull, but Martha found a hope and a joy that was deep and strong. In spite of the scant opportunity she had to learn more of the things of Christ, she was growing in grace. It has always been to me a matter of greatest encouragement to see the faithfulness of the Holy Spirit in leading and teaching these simple believers. The missionary and native evangelists have the responsibility for not one but for a large number of villages. And so when the Lord works and saves souls in different villages we are able to give them only very rare opportunities for learning the things of God. Even with the neglect of yet unevangelized villages we can hardly visit our believers more than once every three or four months.

On the occasion of our first visit to Ghasm after the conversion of Martha she said to me, "Brother Freed, I want your advice on a problem in my life." Then she told me about her engagement to a young man and that the Lord had been speaking to her and telling her that it was wrong for her to marry him. She added, "You have no idea, Brother Freed, what it would mean if I refused to marry him." Now up to that time Martha had never had any teaching on the truth of the unequal yoke of believer with unbeliever and secretly my heart rejoiced to know that the Holy Spirit had revealed to her this vital truth. But to take a stand against this engagement was a very grave matter.

Engagements and marriages among the Arab people are matters of social and business arrangements entered upon by the parents without consulting the children at all. In fact the engagement is often made by the two fathers while their children are still babes in arms. The closer the relation, the greater is the honor and if there should be in the family a boy and a girl, let us say first cousins, of about the same age, the bargain is often made soon after their birth. It actually is a bargain and a strange one, for though otherwise a woman is not considered to be of any worth or value, yet in the marriage transaction she has to be paid for. It is a long drawn-out affair—weeks and months of talking, arguing and even fighting—in which all those interested want to have a share because it adds zest and breaks the monotony of their otherwise rather dull lives. At least the bargain is struck and the price on the girl is usually not set in cash but in such things as a piece of land, so much grain, a certain number of sheep, donkeys or camels, according to the social position of the bride and groom.

Martha was considered to be greatly honored, for she was

engaged to her first cousin, Yousuf. When he became old enough to work he began year by year after each harvest to deliver part of the price. The young man was well on his way to the completion of his part of the contract. After the coming harvest the last payment was expected to be made and then the girl would be his. It was only a few months before the harvest when Martha was saved.

When Martha finished her story I realized fully what was ahead of her. At the same time I could tell by the expression on her face that she had counted the cost and was ready for whatever might happen. She did not need advice; she needed only prayer for grace and strength. We prayed together and I assured her that we and the handful of believers of her village would stand with her though we did not see a way out.

The next day (we learned this several weeks later on our next visit to her village) she told her father that she could not marry Yousuf because she had given her heart to the Lord Jesus Christ and Yousuf was not a Christian. The father, who had already been much agitated during recent weeks because of the change in her manner of life, flew into a rage. He started to beat the girl and kick her. "How dare you refuse the boy of my choosing? Are you going to marry him?" The father was beside himself. Such a thing had never happened to him, nor for that matter to anyone in the village. It was unbelievable that a girl would dare to oppose her father and tell him whom she wanted to marry and whom she did not. The thought of being so disgraced in his community infuriated him. Poor Martha was helpless. "Father, I cannot marry him," was all she could say. Her father would shout and scream and then would start to beat her again until blood was streaming down her face.

Day by day as Martha returned in the evening from the work in the field, her father would start the conversation again and as she would meekly but without hesitation answer, "Father, I cannot," he would beat her. The news spread all over the village, of course, and created indignation everywhere. The Americans had surely poisoned the mind of Martha or hypnotized her, otherwise she would not dare to take such a determined stand against the wish of the father and against the age-old custom of her people. Yes, they all took it upon themselves to show their indignation. When Martha passed her former friends, they would curse and swear and spit at her to show their utter contempt. No one took her side; all were against her except the little band of four or five believers who quietly but fervently prayed for her.

Harvest time was drawing near and Yousuf was making his plans for the last payment—and for the wedding. He boldly announced that the girl was his. If she would willingly marry him so much the better, but he would have her anyway—if necessary by force. In his plan he had not only the consent but the ready assistance of everyone in the village.

And then the harvest was over and the last payment was delivered to Martha's father. The time of the wedding was fixed. It was only a few days before the fateful day that our native evangelist, Barnaba, and I made our next visit to Ghasm. Dear Martha was still hoping and trusting that the Lord would undertake. We were with the believers when the Lord told us to go and see Yousuf, the bridegroom. We knew it was not a simple matter. His wrath was particularly directed toward us for poisoning the mind of Martha and causing him humiliation and trouble. He was all ready for the wedding; the feast was being prepared. This was no time to try to dissuade him from his determined intentions, and yet both of us felt that the Lord wanted us to see him. We asked the believers to pray and we went to his house.

As we entered the courtyard, he saw us and started to curse us at the top of his voice. He called us everything in the category of vile language. Yet bound by the extreme customs of courtesy he invited us in and offered us seats. Our hearts were lifted up to God in prayer and Yousuf quieted down after a while. The Lord gave our Brother Barnaba, a very gifted Egyptian evangelist, words of unusual wisdom and grace. It was not long before the young man was listening with his head hanging down in evident conviction. In a little while he looked up and said, "I know Martha is too good for me. I am not worthy of her; I release her from her obligation. She is free."

There was great rejoicing among the little band of believers.

CHAPTER 15

"And, Behold, the Half Was Not Told"

WHEN the Lord begins a work He completes it. And so it was in the life of Martha, the little Arab girl. The rest of the story is a real romance, written in two lives by the Holy Spirit.

A good many hours away (for the Arabs measure distance by the number of hours it takes to walk it) in another small Arab village, lived Musa. In spite of the fact that he was of marriageable age, Musa had never succeeded in striking a satisfactory bargain for a wife among the people of his own village. To go outside the community in search of a wife would rather lower his social position.

Musa lived in one of the few villages which, in the providence of God, came to receive the Gospel testimony. He be-

came convicted and convinced through the fearless witness of
his brother Mutlak, whose life of suffering and triumph is
related elsewhere in this book. Musa now purposed in his
heart that he would seek a Christian girl for his bride, but
that was not a simple matter. So far as he knew not a single girl in his village or anywhere else had been saved.

One day Musa heard of the wonderful blessings of God
in the far-away village of Ghasm. Reports came to him of
the growing number of believers in that community and of
the unusual grace that was upon them. A friend told him
of the wonderful Sunday sunrise prayer meetings. Musa
longed to attend one of them and so one Saturday night he
started out for Ghasm. It was just about daybreak when he
reached the village. The plowmen were already on their way
to the fields; each man rode donkey-back with the parts of a
wooden plow tied to the side of the animal.

Upon inquiry he located the gathering place of the believers. He expected to await their arrival, but to his surprise they were already meeting and as he entered he found
them on their knees in prayer. Musa joined them and
quietly kneeled. Suddenly he heard something he had never
heard in all his life before. A girl was praying! To Musa
this sounded almost too good to be true. He followed her
prayer and heard the girl pour out her heart to the Lord in
thanksgiving for the wonderful answer and the marvelous
deliverance from some testing unknown to him. As Musa
was absorbed in the wonder of it all the Lord seemed to speak
to his heart that this was the girl for whom he had been
seeking and praying. The girl who so captivated Musa's
imagination was none other than Martha, who had been so
wonderfully delivered from the sufferings and trials of
recent months. It was only a few days ago that God so

miraculously softened Yousuf's heart and set Martha free from her obligation to marry him. Her father, who had so cruelly abused her because of the family disgrace, was thus exonerated. No wonder that Martha's heart was filled with gratitude to her Lord!

The young people met. Arrangements were made and they were married at the mission headquarters in Dera'a where believers from a number of villages gathered to witness and have a part in a wedding that was more like a revival service than a social affair. I consider it one of the joys of my life to have united Musa and Martha in holy matrimony.

When the divine records of the continuation of the Acts of the Apostles shall be revealed, I believe there will be a great place accorded to this little Arab girl who caught the vision of that singleness of heart and purpose which motivated Moses of old, who "by faith . . . when he was come to years, refused to be called the son of Pharaoh's daughter; choosing rather to suffer affliction with the people of God, than to enjoy the pleasures of sin for a season; esteeming the reproach of Christ greater riches than the treasures in Egypt: for he had respect unto the recompence of the reward."

Martha received an earnest of her reward right here on earth.

CHAPTER 16

"Whosoever Drinketh of This Water Shall Thirst"

AS in the days of our Lord, so even today among the Arabs the thought of water and women is inseparable. The village well or pool and the long line of women with their heavy load of water, carried on their heads or shoulders, are still a vital part of the life of the people in the Near East.

Just one well to a village, do you ask? Indeed fortunate are those communities which have one well of good clean water. There are scores of villages not so fortunate. In the province of Hauran, in Syria, for instance, possibly not more than fifteen of the nearly three hundred villages have wells of water, while all the other villages have nothing but open pools for their meager water supply.

These pools which are large, deep holes dug generations ago for this purpose, may be located in the center of the village or on the edge of it. They await the rainy season for their annual replenishing. The rains usually begin in November with a few light showers. In December there are again one or two rainy days. The heavy rains come in January and the first half of February. There are a few rainy days in March and rarely any in April, after which there are no more rains until October or November. For months there is hardly a cloud in the sky.

The early rains are quickly swallowed up by the dry and thirsty land. But when the heavy January and February rains come, the ground becomes saturated and water begins to flow down the mountain sides into the narrow valleys below, which form the dry stony river beds, known as the *wadys*. First there is a trickle of water in them, then a few inches and finally the stream is several feet deep. After some of the torrential rains late in January or early in February, the streams in these *wadys* swell into sizeable rivers and rush and roar with great force toward the plains below.

The swelling of the streams is the occasion for great rejoicing in the villages. News of its sudden arrival is passed excitedly from lip to lip. *El wady ija, el wady ija*—"the stream has come, the stream has come," they cry. Everybody runs to see it. It is the day for which they have been waiting. A crude trench has been prepared to conduct the overflow into the village pool. The stream might pass on the outskirts of the village or it might be two, three or five miles away, and so the canal must be dug for that distance. Now the water freely flows into the pool for some days. When it is full the canal is blocked at its source. Soon the stream itself abates and after two or three weeks only a trickle is left. By March the river bed, with the exception of scattered water holes amid the rocks, is dry again.

The pool is now full and there is the water supply for twelve months. To this pool come the women with their water jugs or containers which are filled by dipping them into the water. To the same pool come the donkeys, sheep and camels to drink. One wonders how these poor people ever survive with such absolute lack of sanitation. However, they are mentally immune, and seem to be physically immune also, to dangers that would stagger us. As time goes on, of course, the condition of the water becomes worse and worse. By the end of summer the pool is only half full and usually a green scum is formed over the top of it. The poor women push the scum aside and dip their jars just the same.

After the heavy rains of early February the fields of grain are a lovely green and on the fallow ground grass and other vegetation appear for a few weeks. The scorching sun and blasting east wind of late March and April would burn up all this grass and so the women have another arduous task. They must gather the grass from the fields and store it for fodder for sheep and donkeys during the dry season.

Early in the morning the women leave their villages in groups with nothing but a large sack for the grass, and for their provision only plain barley bread rolled in a napkin. They may have to walk many miles during the day. They pull the weeds by hand and gradually fill the sacks which are now suspended over their foreheads by the two ends tied together, and hanging down over their backs. Toward sunset they wearily make their way home, with the immense loads towering over their heads.

In the town of Dera'a in Hauran, Mrs. Freed and I would see them daily for a few weeks as they passed our mission home. We were located on the edge of a settlement where merchants and native officials of the province had their dwelling places, while the town itself with its seven thousand peasant farmer population was about a mile away. The last lap of the journey would take them across the river bed and up a steep climb to the top of the hill where the village was situated.

Many times these women would stop at our home for a few moments' rest in the shade of the house. There was no shady place on the way, for there were no trees or large rocks on this flat plateau. And so, when they reached the house in their direct path homeward, they would unload their heavy burdens and rest awhile. Then there would be a knock on the door. We would find a group of them standing there asking for water to drink. Water is scarce and precious but no one would deny it to these poor women.

What a precious opportunity it is, as they stand around awaiting their turn, to tell them about the Lord Jesus who came to offer them "living water"! These poor ignorant women listen to the strange story. They can hardly comprehend what it would mean to never thirst again. Yet one thing they do realize is that it is love that prompts us. Words of kindness are new to them.

But among those listening, there might be one who realizes that we are telling them about a religion different from that of their husbands, and she is frightened. She whispers to the other women, "Don't listen to these Americans; they are telling you about a false religion. God's curse will be upon us. Our children and animals will die; our crops will fail.

And if our husbands find out they will surely beat us."
They look at each other in fear and distress. Some run
to their bundles, put them on their backs and hurry across
the field without even waiting for their turn to drink.

Poor, ignorant souls driven from us by superstition and
fear! They are actually running from the Living Water! It
reminds us of the words of the Lord Jesus to the woman of
Samaria, "If thou knewest the gift of God . . . thou wouldest
have asked . . ." But they do not know; they do not comprehend. They think that we will bring calamity to them and
do not realize that we are offering them the greatest thing
on earth—the gift of eternal life. And so they go away
weary and worn, tired and thirsty in body and in soul.

Are there any among such women who have drunk of
the living waters? Yes, indeed there are!

CHAPTER 17

"Give Me This Water, That I Thirst Not"

A FTER several months of absence it was essential that I should visit again the village of Aera where we had a group of believers. With no trained pastor to shepherd the flock, their simple gatherings week after week would naturally take the form of an enlarged family worship and prayer meeting. Many neglected villages call for our time, yet we become somewhat anxious for the spiritual welfare of these small groups of believers and visit them as often as possible.

The room in which we gathered for a meeting on my arrival in the village was now well filled with a number of unsaved men and women besides the believers, among them some whom I had not seen before.

Nyack College Library

After singing hymns and choruses and reading the Word, I was just about ready to break the Bread of Life to them when from the far, dark corner of the room, where the women usually sit, the voice of a woman rang out. "Brother Freed," she said, "please forgive me, but I cannot keep still any longer. I want to tell you what the Lord has done for me." The woman was a stranger to me. Of course I was happy to have such an interruption and told her to go ahead. "The Lord saved me since your last visit to us and this is how it happened." With this introduction she proceeded to tell a most remarkable story.

Her name was Salameh. Although she had lived in sin and cared nothing about God, she always had a secret longing for some kind of peace and happiness that she did not have nor did she know how to obtain it. One night she had a dream in which it seemed that she went to the village pool as usual to wash her clothes. She rubbed them, scrubbed them and beat them on the rocks but strangely the harder she worked the dirtier the clothes became. Finally in her desperation she cried out to God, whose Name she had used before only in profanity. "O God, help me! I cannot get my clothes clean!" Instantly, in her dream, a person in beautiful white garments appeared and with his arms outstretched said, "Let me have your clothes. I'll make them clean." He took her old dirty clothes and in a moment handed them back to her. Now they were pure and spotless and snow-white. Then he disappeared.

When Salameh awakened she was greatly troubled. She did not understand the dream. With her ignorant superstitious mind she could think only that calamity was about to visit her home. She went to the neighbors and told them of her strange dream, but no one could help her. For weeks afterward whenever she met anyone she would tell her dream, for she still hoped to get an explanation.

One day she was telling her dream to another woman of the village. "I think I know who could help you with your dream," the woman said to her. "Ever since those accursed Americans have come to our village there is a woman who has become very strange. She talks all the time about God and Christ. She will not lie nor curse. She says she knows she is going to heaven. She even tries to learn to read so she can read the Americans' Bible which the priest forbade our husbands to read. Maybe she can help you."

Salameh went to see this strange person who was one of our believers, saved from the darkness of Catholicism some months before. When this woman heard the story, she understood it at once. She explained to Salameh that the person who appeared to her in her dream was none other than the Lord Jesus Christ Himself. The filthy clothes represented her black sinful heart. The Lord had tried to tell her that she could never get her own heart clean no matter how she would try, but if she gave her heart to Him, He would cleanse it in His precious blood and make it white as snow. She told about the joy and peace she had in her heart. Salameh immediately realized that this strange woman did understand the dream and so with mind and heart wide open she listened eagerly. This dear believer not only explained the dream but led her to the Lord right then and there.

No wonder Salameh, filled with joy for her newly found Lord, could wait no longer to tell me her story. After she finished her testimony, with face and hands lifted toward heaven, she gave thanks to the Lord for His mercy and grace. The presence of the Lord was very real. One after another the believers gave testimonies, offered prayers to God and sang His praises. I never gave the message I had planned for the meeting. The Lord had His way in that memorable gathering. Salameh drank of the Fountain of Life deeply; she was satisfied.

CHAPTER 18

"They Shall ... Neither Thirst Any More"

THE experiences of the closing months of 1932 will always linger with me. The rains of January and February of that year were unusually light. The streams which normally swell to great magnitude in February were considerably below the usual level. During the weeks when the swift current of other years would have filled the village pools with fresh water in a very short time, this year only a slow trickling of water passed through the canals in the Hauran. In a number of villages the people became desperate. Men dug new trenches many miles long to other *wadys* of higher altitude to divert more water to the pools. Some were more successful than others. By the time the rains were over there were, particularly in the southeastern portion of the province, fifty or sixty villages with only partially filled pools.

Life continued normally for some months but when October and November came, these pools, which in other years would have some water left in them even in February just before the fresh water came, were nearly exhausted. In December a number of pools were empty, though there were two months yet to go before the new stream would bring relief. In those days I saw women descend into the muddy, slimy bottom of the pools and dig out a circle of the filthy mud two or three feet in diameter and depth. Then they would wait for the water to seep through and scoop it up by cupfuls. It was a pitiful sight. But soon even that was impossible and the bottoms of the pools were as dry as a bone.

What could the poor people do? There was only one source of relief during those long weeks. They had to go to the nearest village which had water, and they were very few. In some cases they had to travel four to five hours each way. You will recall that distance among the village Arabs is always expressed by the number of hours it takes to walk it. During those weeks one could see long lines of donkeys or camels coming from every direction to the privileged village. Four water containers—two on either side—would be fastened on the beast of burden; there would be small ones on the donkeys and large ones on the camels. Hours of travel and hours of waiting at the destination filled the day—and for only a little water. The animals were exhausted from the extra burden placed upon them. The donkeys, which are not as hardy as the camels, suffered particularly from weariness and lack of water. I have seen donkeys which had successfully made the journey to the well with the empty containers, fairly stagger under the load on the return trip and finally

drop dead in their tracks. Thus all the precious water
would be spilled.

The village of Ghasm, where we had a small group of
believers, suffered with the rest. A small branch line of the
Damascus-Transjordan Pilgrim Railway passed through it.
There was a train three times a week. The poor women,
hoping to save themselves the long journey to the village
with the well, would gather at the station early in the morning on the days when the train was due. When it pulled into
the station hundreds of the women with their jars and cans
would storm the engine, and shout and scream and beg
the engineer for water. They knew that he carried a water
supply for the locomotive, but of course he could not give
them water. After a few minutes the train would leave
and the poor disillusioned women would stand with their
empty vessels and stare at the passing train. Yet on the
third day they would be there again, hoping against hope
to obtain water so they would not have to make the long
trip that day.

One morning a dear old woman, one of our believers,
was with the crowd of women at the station. There were
only three or four saved women in the village. The Lord's
mercy and grace had reached Um Yousuf at an age when,
measured by human standards, these women with their minds
dulled and hearts hardened by sin seem to be beyond the
hope of salvation. Yet Um Yousuf drank of the Water of Life
and was satisfied.

She was happy in the Lord, but she was just as wretchedly
poor as the rest of the women and she needed water just the
same. She was too old to go to another village so she went
to the station with her vessel in the hope of getting water.

The train arrived; the screaming women crowded around

the engine as usual. The whistle blew and the train started, leaving the women staring at it as it went on. On this morning, however, a freight car had to be left behind to be loaded with grain. So the train went ahead a short distance, stopped, whistled again and started back. The women who were still standing on the track did not realize what was happening until the train was right upon them. Another sharp whistle brought them to their senses. They jumped and scattered in every direction. Um Yousuf was too old to run. She was caught between the last freight car and the loading platform and in a moment life was crushed out of her.

The sad news of her tragic death was brought to us by a messenger the same day. Fortunately I was at my main station and was able to make ready without delay for this sad mission to the village of Ghasm. There was no time to lose because the dead must be buried the same day. This was to be our first funeral as she was the first believer to die, not only the first in that village but in the whole area. And how sad it was that she had died in an attempt to get a little water!

On the way I looked to the Lord for a message. I realized that not only the believers but many others would attend—members of the family and those who would come out of curiosity to see how we would perform the last rites. The Lord gave me the words from verses sixteen and seventeen in the seventh chapter of Revelation: "They shall hunger no more; neither thirst any more; neither shall the sun light on them, nor any heat. For the Lamb which is in the midst of the throne shall feed them, and shall lead them unto living fountains of waters: and God shall wipe away all tears from their eyes."

As I stood before the body of Um Yousuf wrapped in a

crude cotton sheet to be laid in a gruesome, stone-lined grave with no grass or trees around, no coffin or flowers, my own heart was filled with thanksgiving and gratitude to our Lord as I spoke of the realities of the heavenly home to which she had departed. Yes, she died in wretchedness and misery as she tried to get a little water, but now it was well with her soul. She would never thirst again, for the Lord Himself was leading her unto living fountains of water. Oh, if we had failed to go to that wilderness to tell her of the Living Waters!

CHAPTER 19

"When the Sun Was Up, They Were Scorched"

WHEN Edouard, the Lebanese interpreter of the French Governor, was saved from Catholicism, a new door of testimony was opened to us among the Arab officials and the élite of the town of Dera'a. Edouard had many friends yet he took an uncompromising stand with the despised Protestants.

On Sundays there was always quite a procession of French and native Catholics who passed our mission house on their way to the Catholic church. For Edouard to part from the company of friends and seen by everyone, walk into our service, was a brave act which easily could have had disastrous consequences but for the faithfulness of the Lord.

Among his many friends was Abdul Razzak Beyk, the

only trained dentist in the entire province, a graduate of the French Medical College of Damascus and son of one of the most prominent and influential Moslem families of that great city. Edouard's quiet personal testimony awakened curiosity in Abdul Razzak Beyk to meet us. They came to our house one evening and we had a profitable conversation. Soon the visits became almost nightly and before long the casual conversations were turned into Bible studies. The Bible was an absolutely strange book to this son of a very devout Moslem father. Abdul Razzak Beyk realized that he was now treading on dangerous ground but he was fascinated by the Word and continued to come, in spite of the fact that his other friends became rather agitated by his frequent visits to us.

The work of the Holy Spirit was quiet but deep in this sincere, seeking heart. Several months passed and we realized that Abdul Razzak Beyk was convicted by and convinced of the truth as it is in Christ Jesus. There was no reason to delay any longer. In the presence of Edouard I dealt with him clearly and earnestly about the necessity of giving his heart to the Lord by confessing his sins and accepting the cleansing blood of Christ. His conversion was very evident. He rose from his knees, and as near as one can ever tell he was a born-again child of God. He went away that night rejoicing in Him.

Weeks passed and Abdul Razzak Beyk continued faithfully. How happy we were to see his open testimony! On Sunday morning he would close his office and walk to our meeting under the observation of all his friends. We expected a wave of persecution to break out at any moment but he was kept from it for a while.

As time went on we presented to him the teaching of the

Word of God concerning baptism as a public testimony of his faith in Christ. Abdul Razzak Beyk showed the same openness and willingness to take this step as he had shown when we dealt with him about conversion.

It was a happy occasion when in the river bed on the edge of the town one lovely spring morning he and several others were buried in the waters of baptism.

Still there were no signs of persecution except indignant talk and criticism on the part of the native officials of the community. It continued this way for several weeks. We were really amazed at the comparative tranquillity.

Then our little family left for Damascus where we planned to spend several days. On our return home our native evangelist David met us at the station. He did not have to speak. His expression revealed that something serious had happened during our absence. "Abdul Razzak Beyk took poison or was poisoned yesterday and was taken in a critical condition to Damascus," were David's first words. The whole town was in a turmoil. However, God kept us from any serious trouble. For months we heard nothing about Abdul Razzak Beyk, except that his life was spared and that he was convalescing in his father's home in Damascus. Oh, how we prayed for this dear brother in Christ!

One day we heard that he was back again in Dera'a in his former apartment and that he had reopened his dentist office. We waited for a while, and then Brother David and I took courage and visited him in his home. He gave us a friendly reception, remembered us by name and inquired about our families. There was a strange, far-away look on his face though his conversation was quite normal. When I tried to talk to him about the Lord he spoke in a passive, unemotional way and said that his faith in the Lord had given him joy and peace before, but the way was too hard and the price too great. He asked us to let him alone. The one outstanding conviction I received from our conversation was that there was no willful turning away from the Lord on his part but that some strange influence had robbed him of his will power to press on. Some of us could not help but associate the poisoning with his mental attitude.

We cannot close this story with a note of triumph as we have the others. Years have passed and no new word has been received concerning Abdul Razzak Beyk. He was the victim of a violent ray of the sun of fiery persecution, was scorched and seemingly withered away . . .

CHAPTER 20

"If the Son...Shall Make You Free..."

THERE was a cloud hanging over the small group of earnest, consecrated believers in the village of Ghasm. They were zealous for the life and testimony of each Christian, lest the unsaved should have occasion to reproach them. Yet there was one of their number who did not walk in the full light of the Gospel.

This member was Agaail, the most prominent merchant of the community. When he had been saved every believer greatly rejoiced for the victory won and for the expected influence of this newly transformed life on others. Agaail walked well for a while but now the believers began to notice that he was losing interest and that some of the habits of his old life were returning—habits such as worldly

friendships, questionable dealings in business, withholding
of tithes and smoking.

On the occasion of my next visit to the village I took the
opportunity to speak to Agaail about these things, especially
in view of the fact that he had given them all up previously and had testified of victories, deliverances and blessings. The lack of joy and real love for the Lord were evident
since his backsliding, yet Agaail insisted that he loved the
Lord the same as ever and that there was nothing between him
and the Lord. When we talked to him about the matter of
returning to smoking, he resented the criticism. He told me
that he could see no harm in it and that it did not mar his
fellowship with the Lord. Before I left I quoted to him
the verse in the Gospel of John, "If the Son therefore shall
make you free, ye shall be free indeed." Agaail smiled
and said, "That verse certainly does not apply to me. If I
thought smoking was displeasing to the Lord, I could easily
quit it."

On my periodical visits I would see Agaail. He was very
friendly and a generous host to me, but one could easily
see that he was not where he ought to be with the Lord. The
believers were greatly burdened and prayed much for the
Lord to undertake.

It was now nearly a year· since my conversation with
Agaail. On my next visit I had hardly entered the meeting
room where the Christians were gathered for Sunday morning worship, when I noticed Agaail and I knew instantly
that the Lord had wonderfully undertaken for him. Joy was
written all over his countenance. He was not slow to give
his testimony, which, of course, the believers had already
heard.

A few weeks before my visit Agaail made ready for his

periodical trip to the Bedouin camp which at a certain season of the year was located in that vicinity. It was about five hours' travel on horseback. He bought camel hair, goat skins, goats' butter and other produce from the Bedouins and in exchange he supplied them with wheat, barley, coffee, sugar, matches, etc.

Agaail was nearly an hour's journey on his way when he reached into his saddlebag to get his tobacco and paper to roll himself a cigarette and discovered that his hired man had failed to put them in the bag. He was somewhat annoyed but dismissed the matter from his mind. A half hour later he mechanically reached again into his saddlebag for the tobacco. He was getting restless by this time. Should he return home for it? "Never mind," he said to himself, "I cannot spare the time that would be required to return home and start the journey all over again. I'll wait until I get to the Bedouin camp. They'll give me tobacco. Besides the whole matter is not of such importance."

So he went on. He went past the halfway mark of his trip but by this time he was desperate, as he told us in his testimony. It was too late to return home yet the camp was still some two hours ride away. He just could not stand it that long without a cigarette. As he was in this pitiful plight, suddenly the words of the Scripture which I had quoted to him nearly a year ago came to his mind, "If the Son therefore shall make you free, ye shall be free indeed." He then realized the awful bondage of this habit. He alighted from his horse and right there under God's sky dropped on his knees and asked the Lord to deliver him and set him free.

The Lord instantly answered prayer. He reached the camp without a trace of desire for smoking. He never asked the

Bedouins for tobacco.   This experience put a new love for
the Lord in his heart—an experience to which he gave free
expression in his testimony on that Lord's Day morning, as
we rejoiced together in another triumph of His grace and
power.

CHAPTER 21

"For Where Your Treasure Is..."

G HATTAS was the second richest man in his community and well known throughout the province. He was famed for his hospitality and for his uprightness in business dealings.

When he became a Christian, everything he was and everything he possessed was consecrated to the Lord. One of his first acts was to call in his most loyal and devoted hired helper. He told him that for years he had been cheating him in his wages. He told him that he had lied to him about the crops which were the basis for figuring his wages, and that when he went to sell grain on this helper's account to provide him with cash, he invariably had cheated him on the price received. The hired man could not believe his ears.

He first thought that his master had become mentally un-
balanced. But as he saw the great change in his life day by
day he himself became convicted and was wonderfully saved.

The home of Ghattas became a sanctuary. It had been one
of the most popular places for *sahrah* for years. Evening
gatherings after the day's labors on the field are the only
social functions of the village Arab men. The prosperous
pride themselves in their ability to make these *sahrahs* popular. The main attraction, of course, is the serving of coffee.
The men will sit around the hot coals on which the coffeepot
is kept, and talk over the gossip of the day. Two things
would distinguish a host in connection: absolutely freshly
roasted and prepared coffee every evening, and ability to
serve it throughout the evening without cessation until the
last guest has left.

There is skill in the preparation, and the host will not
leave it to any other member of the family. The fire is
started the minute he returns from the field of labor.
There is in the corner of the guest chamber a large supply
of dry twigs and roots which the women have gathered from
the fields. A few of these are first put on the fireplace which
is simply an indentation, three or four feet square, in the
center of the mud floor. It is about six inches deep and
lined with flat stones so that the ashes can be kept within
its bounds. On top of the twigs, which serve as kindling
wood, are now placed four or five lumps which look like
clay; they are about the size of two fists. These lumps are
dried manure mixed with straw. The preparation of this
fuel is also one of the tasks of the women. They go out in
the field, following the camel and cattle paths, gather up the
refuse and put it in a flat basket which they carry on the top
of their heads. At home they mix it with straw, kneading it

with their hands, and then form it into cakes and dry them in the sun. Finally, they are brought into the room and piled in a corner.

The host is now ready to start the fire. You would not want to be in the room if you could possibly avoid it, at least not for a while. When the fire is started the smoke begins to ascend in clouds. There is no chimney through which it can escape, nor any windows. The only outlet is the door, which is opened after the room has been filled with smoke and stench. If you are patient enough, you will discover that the worst of the smoke rises to the upper half of the room and that after the cakes become red hot they are like charcoal. You are now glad that you are not required to sit on a chair or a davenport but on the floor, because the lower you sit the less likely that your head will be in the clouds of smoke.

The work of preparing the coffee now begins. The bag of green coffee beans is kept with all other valuables in the treasure chest which is the only piece of furniture in the room. The supply that is desired for the evening is placed in an iron skillet with a long handle and is roasted over the fire. This is then put into the coffee urn, which is the pride of the home. It is made of very heavy ebony wood and is round—about ten or twelve inches in diameter and possibly eighteen inches high. In the center is a hole the size of one's fist; this reaches about halfway down into the urn. A long stick, something like a baseball bat and smaller than the hole, completes the equipment. Now the music begins. The men acquire great skill in beating the coffee beans against the sides of the hole in perfect rhythm and they keep on until the coffee is broken up. This wood urn has a good loud ring which can be heard quite a distance across the village. It is the gong announcing that coffee is prepared and everybody is welcome.

As neighbors and friends gather, the brass coffeepot is already imbedded in the red coals, filled with coffee grounds and water which must come to the boiling point several times to give the coffee a thick syruplike substance, as bitter as gall. During the rest of the evening the coffeepot is set in the hot ashes. There is only one cup used for serving. It is a small porcelain cup about the size of our demi-tasse but without a handle. The host squats by the fire where he can be always at the coffeepot and at the same time reach all of the guests who are sitting around in a circle. He pours about one spoonful of coffee into the cup and hands it to the guest of honor who sips it noisily to let the host know how delicious it is, and hands the cup back. It is refilled and handed to the next guest. And so the cup makes the rounds. Then the generous host who desires to establish a reputation for real hospitality, will keep the cup going at a slow pace all during the evening until the last guest is gone. And, of course, one is never supposed to refuse no matter how many times his turn may come.

It was a joy to see how Ghattas would make opportunities during the *sahrahs* to change the conversation to spiritual matters. He would turn the arguments to Bible reading by making the Word of God the basis for settling arguments. Before the people realized it, they themselves acquired the habit of calling for the Bible to see what it had to say on a given subject. These gatherings laid a wonderful groundwork for the harvest of precious souls which inevitably followed.

There was one phase of the Christian life which up to this time had been neglected among the few scattered believers.

This was the giving of tithes to the Lord. The general feeling
had been that these believers were too poor to give anything in the way of material things. Most of them merely
eked out an existence and it was thought cruel to ask them to
give up a portion of this minimum from which they really
could not spare a thing. However, the Lord kept before our
minds the precious promises of His Word, such as "Bring ye
all the tithes into the storehouse . . . and prove me now herewith, saith the Lord of hosts, if I will not open you the windows of heaven, and pour you out a blessing . . ." He
seemed to tell us that we would not deprive the poor believers of bare necessities but on the contrary were cheating them out of blessings which the Lord had in store for
them.

We began to speak to Ghattas and the others and to teach
them from the Word the blessedness of giving. When Christians are yielded and hungry for God's blessing it is easy to
lead them on and soon there was talk everywhere that they
should give the tithe to the Lord at the next harvest. They began to pray for a good harvest so that the Lord's portion
might be as large as possible. One of the rooms was vacated
for storing the grain as it was brought to the Lord.

The hard work of the harvest was now over and the grain
lay on the threshing floors. This is always a time of rejoicing
in the villages. Each family has a threshing floor. They are
like so many vacant lots encircling the village, and are
separated by low stone fences. The grain is brought in on
camel back and spread out on the threshing floor. The
men's work is now about over; the threshing is done by the
boys. A heavy wooden board about three by four feet in
size and studded on the bottom with sharp stones is hitched
to the donkey or camel and the boys ride them around in

circles as on a surf-board, thus crushing out the grain. Following this work comes the winnowing and then the large pile of clear grain is put into sacks.

Threshing time is a very good time for ministries and fellowship with believers individually and by families. They spend most of the day on their threshing floors with very little to do for several weeks but to oversee the work and watch the grain. It is a time I always enjoyed.

It was the first harvest for the Lord's tithe in Ghasm. As I visited the village I found the believers gathered in the meeting room for an important business conference. I entered the room just as they were making up the list and figuring out the prospective tithes. Everybody knew the size of everybody else's land and the possible yield. "We'll put Yousuf down for twenty mudds of wheat and thirty-five mudds of barley. Isn't that about right, Yousuf? Ibrahim, what do you think you will be able to give?" and so on. Then they came to Ghattas. One of the believers spoke up. "He should be able to give about one hundred and fifty mudds of wheat and three hundred mudds of barley." Ghattas appeared to be quite excited and fairly shouted, "That's not right!" My heart sank within me. Was there going to be bargaining among them and would Ghattas of all people be unwilling to give his full tithe because it came to so much more than the share of the others? But my dismay lasted only for a moment, for Ghattas continued, "I am sure that Ibrahim is wrong. I believe my tithe will be at least two hundred mudds of wheat and possibly three hundred fifty mudds of barley." How my heart leaped for joy! Ghattas was not to be cheated out of a blessing.

After the winnowing, the head of the family takes charge on the threshing floor. He squats beside the large pile of grain with an empty sack held by one of the boys, and begins to measure. A wooden pail about the size of a deep four or five quart stewpan is the standard measurement. It represents a quarter of a mudd. He dips it into the grain, then sets it down. Now he takes grain in both of his hands and pours it on the top. He repeats the operation several times until the cup is running over, and then dumps it in the sack.

The believers adapted the custom of having two sacks. Nine measures of grain go into one sack and the tenth into the Lord's bag. When full it is placed on a donkey's back and carried to the floor of the Lord's storeroom where it is dumped. Later on it is sold and the money used for the work of the Lord.

Did the believers suffer because of giving the tithe from their abject poverty? Come and see! God challenged them, "Prove me now herewith . . ." and fulfilled His promise, "I will . . . open you the windows of heaven, and pour you out a blessing . . ."

CHAPTER 22

"But We Have This Treasure in Earthen Vessels"

EARTHEN vessels are among the most ordinary and yet most useful articles in the simple Arab home. In the midst of real poverty and though satisfied with the bare necessities of life, one thing every Arab expects in his own home or in any other home where he may step uninvited is a drink of cool refreshing water. And he will find it, too, for the earthen vessel which can be bought for a few coppers by the poorest person serves remarkably well for the purpose.

This earthen vessel is usually the size of an American water pitcher, and is crudely formed on the potter's wheel. It is large, round on the bottom, and is shaped to a long narrow neck with a small spout protruding on one side near the top. The water is poured into it and then it is set outdoors, generally in the shade where the wind may strike it. If you watch it now you will soon notice trickles of water running down on the bulging, sand-colored sides of the vessel. Though the air is hot outdoors, the water in the jug gets cooler and cooler until after an hour or so you would be surprised how cool it has become. The trickles of water continue in very much the same manner as perspiration forms on the forehead on a hot summer day after one has drunk a great deal of water. It is the simple principle of evaporation which cools the water on the inside.

At all times one is welcome to step into an Arab home and ask or simply reach for the water jug. No drinking glass is needed because you pick up the jug, hold it high in the air without letting it touch your lips, tip it and let the stream through the spout flow freely into your wide-open mouth. It sounds simple, doesn't it? Try it!

But these earthen vessels have another use in some of the more prosperous village homes. Enterprising native artists will take the crude drab-looking vessels and paint the entire jug with gayly colored designs. You would say it is rather primitive art, yet it makes the jars bright, cheery spots in the otherwise dull, gloomy homes. Of course these painted jars are more expensive and you will not find them in many homes.

The proud owner will drive two pegs into the mud plaster of the wall and will put a cardboard or piece of tin on it to serve as a shelf. Then the vessel, now promoted to the function of a vase, is set on it to decorate the home.

But I want to let you in on a little secret. Take the beautifully painted vessel and fill it with water. Set it out on the ground as you do the other vessel and wait. Five, ten minutes pass, half an hour, but no trickle of water appears

on the outside of the vessel. Pick it up and try to drink
the water. You will find it is lukewarm and you will spew
the first swallow of it out of your mouth. The reason is
simple. The paint stops up the pores of the clay and pre-
vents evaporation and cooling.

The application of the figure by the Apostle Paul is
clear. This treasure—"the light of the knowledge of the
glory of God in the face of Jesus Christ"—the Lord would
place in simple, yielded, porous vessels, not for self-display
or vain glory like the painted vessel, but that we may be like
cooling water to the thirsty soul, so "that the excellency of
the power may be of God, and not of us."

Such an earthen vessel was Rifka, an Arab girl of
Ghasm. One day, just as Mrs. Freed and I were preparing
for a preaching trip to the town of Ezraa, Rifka came from
her village to visit us. She was glad to join us on our journey.

On our arrival in Ezraa we went to the house of a friend
where we had held meetings before. It was a difficult place
to go for Gospel testimony. Half of the population were
Moslem and the other half Orthodox and Catholic Arabs.
The chief of the town (it was one of the large communities
of Hauran) was a very bigoted Catholic and in him the
Moslem population found as zealous an opponent to the Gospel as they themselves were.

We reached the town in the late afternoon when the men
were back from their fields of labor and it did not take long
to gather an audience. When we drive into a village with
our car we kick up enough dust, both literally and figur-
atively speaking, that our presence does not need any further announcement. The boys of the village are first on the
scene and they flock around the car like a swarm of bees.
When we first started our village work in the Near East we

were worried and spent a great deal of energy in our efforts
to keep the children off the car. It was particularly hard
to see them use the nicely polished body of the car for a
school board as they worked their mathematical problems
and drew their geometrical designs on the paint of the car
with sharp stones. However, we soon overcame our fretting
for we realized that the Lord would rather have us preserve
our nerves than the smooth enamel of our car. We were
now satisfied if they left the engine and steering gear intact
so that we could transport ourselves, our supplies and our
drinking water.

Eventually we reached our friend's home, and soon the
room was filled in the usual fashion. We were given the
place of honor against the wall opposite the door. Folded
quilts were spread out to form a kind of couch six to eight
inches high with several hard pillows to recline on. On either
side of us a few more quilts were spread for the more important people—men only—while the rest of the men would sit
around and in front of us on thin reed mattings. In the far
end of the room on the bare, hard-rolled, mud-plastered
floor sat a number of women. Lady missionaries are always
accorded a seat of honor with us, and in this case, according
to rules of Arab hospitality, Rifka, since she was our guest,
was placed next to Mrs. Freed. This, however, is a thing
rarely done.

Just before the meeting began, to my great surprise the
chief of the village came in. Everybody stood up until he
was seated to my right, while Mrs. Freed and then Rifka
were to my left. The chief's facial expression boded nothing
good, though according to Arab hospitality he was restrained
at first. Then he engaged in friendly conversation with me,

and inquired about my health and the well-being of my wife, children and all.

We began the meeting by trying to teach them Gospel songs. The chief's face was cold and hard. I now opened my Bible and was about to stand up to preach when Rifka leaned over Mrs. Freed toward me and whispered, "Brother Freed, I believe the Lord wants me to give my testimony." Under normal circumstances among unsaved people, especially with the chief of the village present, Rifka's proposal would have been an impossibility. A woman would not dare to speak in public nor would such a thing be tolerated for a moment by the men. I quickly surveyed the situation. I felt that the Lord was pressing Rifka for a testimony. I also realized that she, being our guest, was to be accorded the same courtesy that Mrs. Freed or I had. I whispered back to her, "Go ahead."

Rifka stood up and began to speak. A glance at the chief was enough. His face turned pale with anger. His eyes were flashing as though he were ready to do anything to punish Rifka. Yet he was a man of dignity and bound by his own customs; he could do nothing but listen. Rifka's face was lit up with the glory of heaven as she gave her testimony. The Lord indeed put words in those illiterate lips. Her testimony lasted several minutes and then she sat down.

There was a strange, tense silence in the room. Every eye was on the chief to see what he would do. Suddenly he stood up, stepped as close to me as he could and pointing his finger toward me said, "Do you know what was the purpose of my coming to your meeting? I determined to see for myself and then put a stop to the preaching of your American religion to my people. Then when this girl"—he pointed at Rifka—"stood up, it was more than I could stand. The idea of her daring to stand up before us and speak. I was going to grab her by the neck and throw her out. But she was your guest and I could not do it. As she spoke, however, I could not believe my own ears. Such beautiful words from the lips of one of our ignorant Arab village girls who normally cannot put a sentence together straight. The more I listened the more I was amazed and realized that God was speaking through her. And now I want to tell you that if this is what your preaching does to our women I am glad you came and you are welcome to come back again." Placing his left hand on his breast and deeply bowing in most cordial greeting, he left the room.

"But we have this treasure in earthen vessels, that the excellency of the power may be of God, and not of us" (II Corinthians 4:7).

CHAPTER 23

"Pray Ye... the Lord of the Harvest"

THE task of evangelizing the Near East is still ahead. What has been done is a mere beginning. Of the eight million Arabs living in lands where Gospel preaching is permitted, only a small percentage have had the opportunity of hearing the message of Salvation through Christ. There are another eight million Arabs living in Saudi Arabia who cannot even be reached with the Gospel for this country is as yet virtually a closed land to the missionary.

A casual glance at missionary statistics for the Near East might give the impression that these lands have a fair share of missionary forces working under a number of missionary societies. But if we sift these figures down to practical realities, the number will prove to be a mere handful.

First, we must eliminate the missionaries, who are even now working for the church union of nominal Protestants with some of the idolatrous Oriental churches. Then we must count out the missionaries who are not preaching the Gospel which is the power of God unto salvation. Furthermore, we have there representatives of many false sects of the West whose work is worse than nothing. Thus the true, evangelical missionary forces, who are carrying on constructive, aggressive, soul-winning work, are very small indeed.

If these groups are detrimental to the Lord's work here in the homeland, their presence is nothing short of tragic on the mission field. The natives do not understand why two groups of missionaries, both coming from Christian lands, should have two different kinds of beliefs and work in opposition to each other. Often this fact will absolutely close the mind of the native to the message of the Gospel. Are not the already existing difficulties enough?

It has been the experience of missionaries in other parts of the world that it is almost impossible to win Moslems to Christ, and this when scores and hundreds of others around them are accepting the Truth. Combine the extreme impenetrability of the Moslem with the proud, quick-tempered, prejudiced and determined nature of the Arab and the task seems hopeless. Then, too, as shown in a previous chapter, the sin-laden, hardened, debauched and blinded Greek Orthodox Arab is little better. "This situation is hopeless," you may say. But He who trod this very same soil has said, "And other sheep I have, which are not of this fold: them also I must bring . . ."

If, because of years of darkness and degradation, these hardened, bigoted, sinful men have only half an opportunity, then the poor, ignorant, enslaved women have virtually none.

But the Lord Jesus loves their souls and not only does He say that He is ". . . not willing that any should perish . . ." but also "Go ye [for] I am come that they might have life . . ." Truly ". . . the night cometh, when no man can work."

But the work of the Lord goes on. He is gathering out a people for His Name from among the Arabs. Trophies of His grace such as recorded in the preceding chapters are being won by God's faithful ministers, both native and foreign, in increasing numbers. The time is short. The unfinished task demands speedy re-enforcements. "Pray ye therefore the Lord of the harvest, that he would send forth labourers into his harvest" (Luke 10:2).

CHAPTER 24

Epilogue I

OUR first term of service was a long one—from October 1926 till the spring of 1933.

Much of the year of furlough was spent in deputation and conference ministries. Our travels took us, naturally, to Detroit and to the Burroughs Adding Machine Company, where I was anxious to see old friends, both in the offices and in the factory. The years 1933 and 1934 were during the time of the great economic depression in the United States. This was evident at the Burroughs Company. A half-empty office and a greatly reduced force of workers in the factory was a rather disheartening sight. The last call was to Mr. B., General Sales Manager, who was now second in command of the entire organization.

Mr. B. well remembered me, having known some of the circumstances of my resignation in 1923 and of my becoming a missionary. "Tell me what you have been doing since going to the Near East." I related some of my experiences, including one or two stories of conversions. This gave me an excellent opportunity to have an indirect witness by emphasizing the necessity of the new birth and the radical change of life in these converted Arabs. Mr. B., who was a Roman Catholic, listened very attentively. "You know, since you left, my son entered the training of the Jesuit ministry and also expects to eventually go overseas. I am very proud of him."

It was now time to excuse myself, as I heard the noon hour bell. "Come and have lunch with me," said Mr. B., and he took me up to the executive dining room. After the meal we returned to his office, and I again excused myself. He insisted that I stay and tell some more of my experiences. Finally it was time for me to leave. Then he said something that stayed with me as a cherished compliment till this very day. "Ralph, remember that if you should feel like coming back to work with us, there is a good position awaiting you." I said, "Thank you very much, Mr. B., but in these depression years you do not take on new workers; you are laying men off." Mr. B.'s answer was, "Don't you worry about that, there is always a place for you." Then he added, "However, I know you will not take me up on my offer. You are too happy in the work you are doing."

CHAPTER 25

Epilogue II

IN 1946, having been appointed Field Director of the
Near East Mission of the Christian and Missionary Alliance, we moved our residence from the Hauran in Syria to
the city of Jerusalem where our mission had its field headquarters. Those were very busy years for me, spending a
good part of my time visiting our mission stations in Lebanon,
Syria, and Transjordan, encouraging and counseling our
missionaries.

In the meantime, feelings of bitter hostility between Jews
and Arabs grew in intensity, particularly in Jerusalem. This
developed into a great deal of violence and street battles,
with the British Government, who had the mandate over
Palestine and Transjordan, getting into the middle of the fight.

Things went from bad to worse. Many days we would not dare to go outside our own home. Often at night we sat in the well-protected basement of the building listening to shooting all around us. One day a bomb planted in the building next to us, which housed some Government offices, completely destroyed that building and a number of dead and injured were found in the ruins. This explosion also damaged our building, and Mildred was injured.

After this experience Mildred's nerves began to fray, and I soon realized that we must get out of this situation as it was next to impossible to carry on any ministries.

With Arab friends we made arrangements to be taken to Lydda Airport, a two-hour trip in a very mountainous area infested with Arab guerillas. We started out with a convoy of five cars. What a relief it was when we safely arrived at the airport where a plane was waiting to take us to Beirut, Lebanon, and out of the troubled areas. We wondered why we had to wait nearly two hours at the airport; no one would give us any information until after we were finally airborne on the way to Beirut. We learned then that only four out of the five cars arrived at Lydda, and they were waiting for the fifth car. It never arrived. It was blown up and its five passengers killed. How we thanked the Lord for our safe arrival!

From Beirut another plane took us to the island of Cyprus. What an overwhelming feeling was the peace and tranquility of this lovely island! (Years later violence broke out in Cyprus also between its hostile Greek and Turkish population. To this day only an uneasy peace prevails there.) After staying in Cyprus five months, we realized that there seemed no hope of an early settlement between Arabs and Jews. With

heavy hearts we left our chosen field of labor and returned
to the States in 1949.

For almost two years I held a pastorate in a newly established church in Arlington, Virginia, just across the Potomac
River from Washington, D.C. Then I received a call to teach
in the Canadian Bible College in Regina, Saskatchewan.
Here we spent three very happy years. I was now 62 years
old and expected to spend the rest of my active life in this
ministry. But God had still other plans for us.

CHAPTER 26

Epilogue III

MY son Paul, a Youth For Christ evangelist, went to Switzerland to attend the YFC International Crusade. After some days of conference they broke up into teams of two or three, visiting various countries in Europe. Paul's lot was to go to Spain. During the following weeks he became greatly burdened to evangelize the people of Spain where open evangelistic meetings were forbidden. His journeys took him to Tangier, an international city at the tip of North Africa, separated from Spain only by the Strait of Gibraltar. While in Tangier Paul learned of the possibility of broadcasting into Spain through the facilities of a commercial station.

Paul returned to the States with this new burden and vision on his heart. He visited many churches and presented the challenge of reaching Spain by radio. He was encouraged by the interest manifest, but soon became dismayed as pastor after pastor told him, "Paul, we are interested in your plans. Let us know when you get started, and we shall see what we can do to help you." "When you get started. . . ." But how?

Paul always looked to me for advice, and he came all the way from North Carolina to Saskatchewan to unburden his heart to me. "Father, how will I get started? Even apart from funds I would need just the right person to go to Tangier while I present the need here in the States." Then he suddenly turned to me, "Father, I would rather have you and Mother start such a work in Tangier than anyone else I know."

After Paul left, the Lord kept speaking to our hearts. Just a few weeks before Paul's visit, the President of the Bible College had resigned, and I was unanimously elected by the school Board to be his successor. It was now April and I was to assume my new responsibilities at the opening of the new school year in September. It soon became very clear to us that He wanted us to take up the challenge of Tangier. So, to the regret of everyone at the school, I resigned my position. We went to North Carolina in June and remained there till January to make plans for what was to be known as The Voice of Tangier.

I was now under no mission board and had no pledged support. Paul and I made an agreement. Mother and I would go to Tangier as soon as funds for the trip came in. Paul now could tell his pastor friends that we *were starting* broadcasting to Spain. He would send me all gifts coming in for this purpose. Mother and I would keep for our personal use each month funds for our bare necessities, and all the rest would go to the cost of broadcasting into Spain. So we sailed for Tangier in January 1954 and a few months later started to broadcast to Spain in the Spanish language.

For some months we were sorely tested, but the Lord was faithful and the work grew. Language after language was added to our daily schedule. Our staff of workers steadily increased.

We continued until most unexpectedly the International Zone of Tangier became part of the Kingdom of Morocco. One of their first acts was to nationalize all radio, and we were given from April 1959 until the end of the year to close down all of our activities.

In the meantime the Lord was working on our behalf, resulting in the opening of a new and far greater door for us. Through the remarkable leading of the Lord, Paul contacted the management of Radio Monte Carlo, a powerful commercial radio station in Europe. After long negotiations, an agreement was reached to install for Trans World Radio's exclusive use a 100,000 watt transmitter with an array of directional antennas. The system was designed to effectively reach large parts of Europe, North Africa, and the Middle East.

In October 1959 we signed the agreement, and on October 16, 1960 we had our first broadcast on the air. Naturally we could no longer carry on the work under the name of "The Voice of Tangier," so we chose the name "Trans World Radio."

My son Paul, as President of Trans World Radio, and I, as General Director, have worked hand in hand under the blessing of our God with the help of an ever-increasing staff of devoted missionary workers. A very effective story of these developments, beginning with the Tangier days, has been written as an autobiography of Paul under the title *Towers to Eternity*.

When thinking of my father, there is one picture that stands out in my memory more than any other. It is one repeated many times over of him sitting in a small mud-lined stone room in an Arab village. Crowded tightly around him would be the men of the village, with the women in the far recesses of the dingy dark room. In the center is a fire with smoke filling the air. On the fire is a little coffeepot with some of the thick sweet syrup-type coffee. It will be passed around in a single small cup to be sipped by all as a symbol of welcome to the visitors.

Soon he will be speaking to these cold, hardened hearts. The deep furrowed rugged faces, not too clearly visible through the dingy smoke-filled room, will depict the hardness of heart and callousness of a sin-ravaged people. The words will flow with virtually no foreign accent. They will come with the combination of a real knowledge of these people and of what the Lord Jesus Christ can do for them. At some point, it may be in hours, it may be days, or even years, many of those hard faces and even harder hearts will show a miraculous change from death unto life.

To see as a boy the power of the Gospel later written on these faces, and more importantly manifested in their lives, is something I will never forget. To me this was "Reaching Arabs for Christ."

Behind the scenes is the everyday life of a godly man who knows and lives Christ as few do. His total life has been one of honoring the Lord Jesus Christ and making Him known. As his son, I have known him down through the years as few can know him. Truly his has been a life totally and completely dedicated not only to "Reaching Arabs for Christ," but so many many others as well.

Paul